Country Baking

T I M E - L I F E   B O O K S

Alexandria, Virginia

Country Baking

*delicious pies, cakes,
cookies, breads, and more
for all occasions*

A REBUS BOOK

C O N T E N T S

INTRODUCTION

6

Pies

*country pies to top off everyday meals, holiday dinners, and
picnic feasts • fruit pies and pastries for all seasons • butter-and-egg "winter"
pies • regional, Shaker, and Pennsylvania-German specialties • features on
decorative pie crust techniques, making a rustic fruit pie, fried and
make-do pies, and antique glass rolling pins*

8

Cakes

*praiseworthy desserts in the great American
tradition • lofty layer cakes • rolled, upside-down, and ice cream filled
cakes • homey apple, oatmeal, jam, spice, and poppyseed
cakes • irresistible chocolate cakes • features on antique spice
containers, the Pillsbury Bake-Off, and making
candied fruits for cake decorating*

44

Cookies

*baking fun for the whole family • snickerdoodles, hermits,
and other cookie-jar classics • favorite bar cookies, from brownies to
lemon squares • pecan puffs, gingerbread, spritz, and lace cookies for
holidays and parties • features on vintage cookie jars, cookie
molds, making two-tone butter cookies, and royal
icing decorations*

76

Quick Breads, Coffee Cakes, and Muffins

*simple but rewarding treats for breakfasts, snacks, and
teatime · easy-to-bake loaves in a variety of flavors · sweet and savory
muffins for any time of day · rich fruit- and nut-topped coffee
cakes · sweet raised-dough pastries · features on muffin pans,
gas stoves, and making shaped pastries*

Breads, Biscuits, and Crackers

*the staff of life in all its satisfying variety · hearty whole-
grain breads · cheese-laced and herb-flavored loaves and rolls · amusing
flowerpot breads · country-fresh biscuits in a range of regional styles · crunchy
homemade crackers · features on Alaskan sourdough, elegant
dinner rolls, and an impressive ring-shaped bread*

Imagine baking day in a country kitchen of a hundred and fifty years ago. It is early morning and the women have gathered to light the fire in the woodstove and organize the ingredients for making a variety of cookies, cakes, breads, and pies. From a food safe in the cellar come pans of fresh milk and cream, wire baskets brimming with freckled eggs, and stoneware crocks of meadowsweet butter. Yellowware bowls are filled with flour and sugar, and a jelly cupboard yields jars of preserves, walnuts, almonds, raisins, and currants. Baskets of fresh fruits are carried in from outdoors, and the drawers of a spice chest supply precious ground nutmeg, cinnamon, ginger, and cloves. Soon the kitchen is filled with tantalizing aromas.

An idyllic scene? Perhaps. But it is easy to forget that long days of labor have already been spent simply getting these ingredients to the table. Cows have been milked and butter churned; flour has been sieved and nuts shelled. Whole spices have been laboriously ground using mortar and pestle. And even now—on baking day—more hard work remains. The stove, once lit, will require constant attention: wood must be added regularly to keep the oven at an even heat, and it will take an expert baker to judge when the temperature is right. Meanwhile, there is the matter of mixing. Without benefit of an eggbeater, the cook must beat the ingredients using a wooden spoon, a wire whip, or perhaps a small tree branch—a process that can easily take up to an hour.

A modern baker can only shake her head at such tiring and time-consuming tasks. Today, with the availability of a wide variety of labor-saving ingredients and equipment, baking is not only pleasurable but relaxing. Even traditional country recipes, like those offered in this book, require little time or expertise. Indeed, no inborn knack is needed to excel at baking. The key is to use quality ingredients, measure exactly, and follow the directions carefully.

If you have never baked before, start with simple drop cookies and quick breads, and then move on to more complicated techniques, such as making a pie with a decorative border or a filled and rolled cake. When you have the luxury of time, try a yeast bread or an elaborate layer cake. And to prepare for those occasions when cooking time is limited, bake and freeze a supply of rich butter cookies and simple loaf cakes, which keep well and are ideal for short-notice entertaining.

Even with modern conveniences, your baking can still pay homage to the past. Consider using antique muffin tins or cookie molds, or rolling out your dough with a pretty glass rolling pin. And when setting the table, choose vintage linens and tableware to enhance the presentation of your country baked goods, fresh from the oven.

Pies

*the fruits of fields
and orchards enclosed
in golden crusts*

I f one particular food could be said to epitomize American baking, it would surely be pie; in fact, more pie is eaten in this country than in any other. Over the years, the typically American double-crusted pie has come to symbolize all that is wholesome and generous in down-home cooking. Bursting with the fruits of our orchards and fields, freshly baked pies bespeak the bounty of the land and the comforts of the country kitchen.

It is said that New Englanders once ate pie three times a day. But while few New Englanders—or anyone else—would now serve pie at every meal, it is still a favorite dessert for occasions both great and small. "Who can dream of a Thanksgiving dinner without a pie!" wrote Fannie Merritt Farmer in 1896, and her words still ring true today. In this chapter, you will find not only traditional recipes for pies made with apples, blueberries, cranberries, and sweet potatoes, but also some new classics such as peanut butter cup pie and coconut cream pie with a chocolate-coconut crust, both perfectly suited for today's country table.

A hint of orange enlivens a homey Blueberry Pie with Marmalade.

Pastry-Wrapped Pears

Frugal cooks have always saved pastry scraps (left after trimming a pie crust) to concoct homey treats like jam tarts and diminutive dumplings and turnovers. This elegant dessert, suitable for a holiday dinner or other festive meal, expands on the same theme. The pasty-wrapping technique could also be used with apples.

PASTRY
2½ cups flour
2 tablespoons sugar
1 teaspoon salt
1 stick (4 ounces) chilled butter, cut into pieces
5 tablespoons chilled vegetable
   shortening, cut into pieces
8 tablespoons ice water

FILLING AND GLAZE
⅓ cup chopped walnuts
¼ cup apricot preserves
½ teaspoon cinnamon
4 Bosc pears
1 egg yolk
1 tablespoon milk

1. Make the pastry: In a large bowl, combine the flour, sugar, and salt. With a pastry blender or two knives, cut in the butter and shortening until the mixture resembles coarse crumbs.

2. Sprinkle 4 tablespoons of the ice water over the mixture and toss it with a fork. The dough should be just barely moistened, enough so it will hold together when it is formed into a ball. If necessary, add up to 4 tablespoons more water, 1 tablespoon at a time. Divide the dough into 4 pieces, wrap each piece in plastic wrap, and refrigerate for at least 30 minutes.

3. On a lightly floured surface, roll out each piece of dough to a 12 x 10-inch rectangle. From each rectangle, cut a 10 x 10 x 10-inch triangle. Place the triangles on sheets of waxed paper. Cut 16 leaf shapes from the scraps, place them on waxed paper, and use a knife to mark veins on them. Cover the pastry triangles and leaves with plastic wrap and refrigerator them for at least 15 minutes before baking.

4. Meanwhile, make the filling: In a small bowl, stir together the walnuts, preserves, and cinnamon.

5. Without removing the stems, peel the pears. Carefully core each pear from the bottom to within ¾ inch of the stem end, then fill the cavities with the walnut mixture.

6. Line a baking sheet with baking parchment or foil. Lay the pastry triangles on the work surface. Moisten the edges of one triangle with water, then stand a pear in the center of the triangle. Bring the edges of the pastry together to enclose the pear, leaving the stem exposed, and pinch the edges together. Brush the backs of the pastry leaves with water and press them around the tops of the pastry-wrapped pears. Place the pears in the refrigerator for at least 15 minutes before baking.

7. Preheat the oven to 375°.

8. In a small bowl, stir together the egg yolk and milk. Brush the pastry with the egg glaze and bake for 20 to 25 minutes, or until the pastry is lightly browned. Serve the pastry-wrapped pears warm.

Makes 4 pastries

Pastry-Wrapped Pears

Fudge Pie with Gingersnap Crust

Fudge Pie with Gingersnap Crust

Chocolate curls add an elegant finishing touch to this pie. To make the curls, shave the flat side of a chocolate bar with a vegetable peeler, using long, even strokes. For best results, warm the chocolate bar in your hand for a minute or two.

GINGERSNAP CRUST
Thirty-five 2-inch gingersnaps (about 9 ounces)
1 stick (4 ounces) butter, melted
2 tablespoons sugar

FILLING
6 ounces unsweetened chocolate

1 stick (4 ounces) butter
4 eggs
¾ cup (packed) brown sugar
⅔ cup heavy cream
1 teaspoon vanilla extract
Lightly sweetened whipped cream and
*   chocolate curls, for garnish (optional)*

1. Preheat the oven to 325°.

2. Make the crust: Place the gingersnaps in a food processor or blender and process to form fine crumbs. Turn the crumbs into a bowl, add the melted butter and the sugar, and blend well. Press the crumb mixture evenly into a 9-inch pie plate to form a crust; set aside.

3. Make the filling: In a small heavy saucepan, melt the chocolate and butter, and cook over low heat, stirring until smooth. Remove the pan from the heat and set aside to cool.

4. In a large bowl, beat the eggs. Beat in the sugar, then beat in the cooled chocolate mixture. Beat in the ⅔ cup of heavy cream and the vanilla. Pour the filling into the crust and bake for 25 to 30 minutes, or until the filling is just set. The center may still be slightly wobbly.

5. Let the pie cool to room temperature, then slice it into wedges and top each serving with whipped cream and chocolate curls, if desired.   *Makes one 9-inch pie*

Peanut Butter Cup Pie

For the sweet-toothed, peanut butter (your choice of creamy or chunky) and chocolate should prove an irresistible combination. Invented around the turn of the century, peanut butter was popularized at the 1904 St. Louis World's Fair, which reputedly witnessed the debut of two other American food favorites: the hamburger and the ice cream cone.

Gingersnap Crust (see Fudge Pie,
opposite)
3 ounces semisweet chocolate
1 tablespoon butter
1½ cups peanut butter

⅓ cup (packed) brown sugar
1 cup milk
½ cup light cream or half-and-half
1 teaspoon vanilla extract

1. Follow Step 2 of the Fudge Pie recipe to make the Gingersnap Crust.

2. In a small heavy saucepan, melt the chocolate and butter over low heat, stirring until smooth. Remove the pan from the heat and set aside to cool.

3. Make the filling: In a medium bowl, beat the peanut butter until softened and smooth. Gradually beat in the sugar. Add the milk, cream, and vanilla, and continue beating until smooth.

4. Pour the peanut-butter filling into the crust. Pour in the melted chocolate mixture, and gently swirl it through the peanut-butter filling; do not blend completely.

5. Cover the pie with plastic wrap and place in the freezer for at least 6 hours, or overnight.

6. Let the pie stand at room temperature for 15 minutes before serving.

Makes one 9-inch pie

Ginger has been a popular ingredient in American baking since colonial times; in fact, ginger cookies were even used to buy votes in 18th-century Virginia. Most current American cookbooks include soft and hard gingerbreads. Earlier sources reveal recipes for sponge gingerbread; for Muster-day gingerbread, which was served to the local militia on training days; for common, fruit, seed, sugar, and even "polka" gingerbreads; and for ginger crisps, ginger nuts, and, of course, gingersnaps.

GLASS ROLLING PINS

Colorful blown-glass rolling pins were first made in England in the late 18th century. Perhaps because the major glass-makers were located in or near seaports, sailors often bought these decorative rolling pins as souvenirs for their mothers, wives, and sweethearts. Nautical designs or sentimental inscriptions, such as "Be true to me," sometimes adorned these love tokens.

The most renowned producer of glass rolling pins was the Nailsea Glass Works near Bristol, in operation between 1788 and 1873. The word "Nailsea" became synonymous with the style of patterned glass this factory originated, even when the glass was produced far from Bristol, in places such as Yorkshire and Shropshire. The characteristic Nailsea patterns were created by rolling molten glass in colored or white enamel chips. When the glass was reheated and blown into its final shape, the chips became part of the surface design. The ribbony effects, typical of Venetian glass, were probably created by Venetian craftsmen employed by the English factories.

Although intended as souvenirs, the rolling pins could, of course, be used in the kitchen. Some models had corked openings at the ends, which allowed them to be packed with flour for added weight, or to be filled with cracked ice or cold water for rolling pastry in warm weather.

Particularly favored by collectors are patterned glass rolling pins known as "Nailsea;" less flashy etched and plain glass examples are also highly prized.

Cranberry-Pecan Pie with Cornmeal Crust

Instead of pumpkin or mince pie, offer this colorful dessert at Thanksgiving or Christmas dinner, and top it off with a scoop of vanilla ice cream. The refreshingly tart filling, made by combining cranberries with fresh apples, dried apricots, pecans, and maple syrup, tastes like a crunchy cranberry relish. In fact, if the flour is omitted, the fruit and nut mixture can be served as a condiment with poultry or ham.

PASTRY

1 cup flour

1/3 cup yellow cornmeal

2 tablespoons sugar

3/4 teaspoon salt

4 tablespoons chilled butter, cut into pieces

3 tablespoons chilled vegetable shortening, cut into pieces

4 to 5 tablespoons ice water

FILLING AND GLAZE

3 cups cranberries

2 medium Granny Smith or other tart green apples, unpeeled and finely chopped

3/4 cup dried apricots, chopped

3/4 cup chopped pecans

1/3 cup maple syrup

1/4 cup flour

1 egg yolk beaten with 1 tablespoon milk

1/3 cup orange marmalade

1. Make the pastry: In a large bowl, combine the flour, cornmeal, sugar, and salt. With a pastry blender or two knives, cut in the butter and shortening until the mixture resembles coarse crumbs.

2. Sprinkle 2 tablespoons of the ice water over the mixture and toss it with a fork. The dough should be just barely moistened, enough so it will hold together when it is formed into a ball. If necessary, add up to 3 tablespoons more water, 1 tablespoon at a time. Form the dough into a flat disk, wrap in plastic wrap, and refrigerate for at least 30 minutes.

3. On a lightly floured surface, roll the dough out to a 12-inch circle. Fit the dough into a 9-inch glass pie plate. Trim the overhang to an even ½ inch and fold it under; crimp the dough to form a decorative border. Prick the pastry with a fork. Place the pie shell in the freezer to chill for at least 15 minutes before baking.

4. Preheat the oven to 400°.

5. Make the filling: In a food processor, pulsing the machine on and off, coarsely chop the cranberries. Transfer the cranberries to a large bowl, add the apples, apricots, pecans, maple syrup, and flour, and stir until well blended; set aside.

6. Line the pie shell with foil and fill it with pie weights or dried beans. Brush the pie border with the egg-yolk mixture and bake for 10 minutes. Remove the pie shell from the oven and reduce the oven temperature to 375°.

7. Remove the foil and weights from the pie shell and spoon the filling into the shell, spreading it evenly with a spatula. Return the pie to the oven and bake it for another 20 minutes, or until the crust is golden; set aside to cool slightly.

8. In a small saucepan, warm the marmalade over low heat until it is pourable. Spoon the warmed marmalade over the cranberry filling.   *Makes one 9-inch pie*

Today, fresh whole cranberries are widely available in the fall. They can be put directly into the freezer until needed, or bought already frozen. In 1909, however, a household manual recommended that cooks take them "to a cool upstairs place and stir lightly with the hand occasionally, till dry; then leave them to freeze, as it happens, and they will keep both color and flavor as long as they last."

Cranberry-Pecan Pie with Cornmeal Crust

Oatmeal Breakfast Pie

Pie once was (and in some parts of the country, still is) eaten as part of a hearty American farm breakfast; this homey pie, made with oats, brown rice, and whole-wheat flour, is a wholesome choice for the first meal of the day. Accompany it with some sliced fruit—peaches would be good—and a little cream. Although the pie tastes best on the day it is baked, few cooks keep farmers' hours and would probably prefer to make the pie the day before. It should be reheated for 20 minutes in a 300° oven.

PASTRY
¾ cup whole-wheat flour
½ cup all-purpose flour
⅓ cup old-fashioned rolled oats
¼ teaspoon baking powder
¼ teaspoon salt
4 tablespoons chilled butter, cut into pieces
3 tablespoons chilled vegetable
   shortening, cut into pieces
4 to 5 tablespoons ice water

FILLING
1½ cups milk
¾ cup cooked brown rice
¼ cup sugar
⅓ cup old-fashioned rolled oats
⅓ cup golden raisins
1 teaspoon vanilla extract
½ teaspoon cinnamon
2 eggs

1. Make the pastry: In a large bowl, combine the flours, rolled oats, baking powder, and salt. With a pastry blender or two knives, cut in the butter and shortening until the mixture resembles coarse crumbs.

2. Sprinkle 2 tablespoons of the ice water over the mixture and toss it with a fork. The dough should be just barely moistened, enough so it will hold together when it is formed into a ball. If necessary, add up to 3 tablespoons more water, 1 tablespoon at a time. Form the dough into a flat disk, wrap in plastic wrap, and refrigerate for at least 30 minutes.

3. On a lightly floured surface, roll the dough out to a 12-inch circle. Fit the dough into a 9-inch glass pie plate. Trim the overhang to an even ½ inch all the way around. Fold the overhang under and crimp the dough to form a decorative border. Prick the pastry with a fork. Place the pie shell in the freezer to chill for at least 15 minutes before baking.

4. Preheat the oven to 400°.

5. Line the pie shell with foil, fill it with pie weights or dried beans, and bake it for 10 minutes. Remove the foil and weights, and set the pie shell aside to cool; reduce the oven temperature to 350°.

6. Make the filling: In a medium saucepan, combine the milk, rice, sugar, rolled oats, raisins, vanilla, and cinnamon, and cook over medium heat just until the mixture thickens and bubbles. Remove the pan from the heat.

7. In a small bowl, lightly beat the eggs. Stir ½ cup of the hot milk mixture into the eggs, then pour the egg mixture back into the milk mixture and stir until well blended. Pour the filling into the pie shell and bake it for 20 minutes, or until the filling is set and dry at the edges. Serve the pie warm.

Makes one 9-inch pie

MAKE-DO PIES

Americans have always hated to give up dessert—especially pie. In times past, when supermarkets did not exist and fruit was only available locally and in season, creative American cooks devised simple substitutes for ingredients they lacked. Their ingenuity resulted in mock apple, mock cherry, mock pecan, and other make-do fillings for pies.

Most Americans are familiar with mock apple pie from the recipe that first graced the back panel of Ritz cracker boxes in the 1940s, and which continued to appear for years thereafter. However, cracker-based mock apple pies have a much longer history in American baking. Enterprising 19th-century cooks contrived a tasty substitute for apples when supplies of the fresh (and dried) fruit ran out. They filled a pastry crust with soda crackers moistened with lemon juice (or vinegar) and a bit of butter, then seasoned them with cinnamon, nutmeg, and other traditional apple pie spices. The crackers plumped up and softened in the baking, and the filling tasted satisfyingly (if surprisingly) like cooked apples.

Over the years ingenious American bakers have created ersatz fillings to approximate the flavors and textures of other favorite pies. For example, a meatless mock mincemeat pie was made by adding rai-

sins, molasses, and cloves to the ever useful soda crackers soaked in vinegar; some variations on the theme used potatoes or green tomatoes in place of crackers.

A mock cherry pie relied on a combination of cranberries and raisins to masquerade as cherries. If fresh lemons were unavailable, a custardy vinegar pie made a convincing substitute for lemon pie. For mock pecan pie, inexpensive dried pinto beans were cooked, chopped, and combined with corn syrup, vanilla, and butter. And for a finishing touch, when there was no cream in the house, some cooks topped their pies, mock or otherwise, with mock whipped cream: beaten egg whites mixed

with confectioners' sugar, grated apples, and vanilla.

To make an old-fashioned soda-cracker mock apple pie, use a double-crust 9-inch pie dough recipe. Roll out the bottom crust and line a pie plate with it. Chill for about 30 minutes, or until firm. Meanwhile, make the filling: Crumble 42 unsalted saltines (a 4-ounce package) into a large bowl; stir in 1 cup chopped walnuts and ½ cup raisins; set aside. In a small pan, combine ¼ cup brown sugar, 1 cup apple juice, 2 tablespoons lemon juice, 1 teaspoon grated lemon zest, and ½ teaspoon cinnamon, and bring to a boil. Boil until the sugar has dissolved and the liquid is clear, 2 to 3 minutes. Remove the pan from the heat, let the mixture cool slightly, then add to the crushed cracker mixture. Turn the filling into the pie shell and dot with 1 tablespoon of butter. Roll out the top crust and lay it over the filling. Trim the overhang to an even ½ inch all the way around. Fold the overhang under and crimp the dough to form a decorative border. Cut several steam vents in the top crust, brush with an egg glaze (1 egg yolk beaten with 1 teaspoon water), and sprinkle with 1 teaspoon granulated sugar. Bake the pie at 400° for 20 minutes, or until the crust is golden.

Marlborough Pie

This winter dessert, also known as apple cream pie, is probably of New England origin. Some recipes call for chopped apples, but most use applesauce, which could be made in the fall and canned, or cooked up as needed from dried apples or from fruit wintered-over in a root cellar. In a pinch, substitute 1½ cups of store-bought chunky applesauce, but omit the sugar and Steps 4 and 5. Stir the lemon juice and cinnamon into the applesauce before proceeding with Step 6.

Pie Pastry (recipe follows)
2 medium Granny Smith or other tart
green apples, peeled and cut into
coarse chunks (about 3 cups)
½ cup sugar

2 tablespoons lemon juice
½ teaspoon cinnamon
3 eggs
¾ cup heavy cream

1. Make the Pie Pastry.
2. Preheat the oven to 300°.
3. Line the pie shell with foil, fill it with pie weights or dried beans, and bake it for 15 minutes. Remove the foil and weights, and set the pie shell aside to cool. Increase the oven temperature to 325°.
4. Make the filling: In a medium saucepan, combine the apples, sugar, lemon juice, and cinnamon, and bring to a simmer over medium heat, stirring to dissolve the sugar. Reduce the heat to low and simmer, partially covered, until the apples can be easily mashed against the side of the pan with a spoon, about 15 minutes.
5. Remove the pan from the heat and mash the apples, leaving them slightly chunky. Set aside to cool slightly.
6. In a large bowl, beat the eggs until thick and lemon-colored. Add the cooled applesauce and cream, and mix thoroughly.
7. Pour the filling into the pie shell and bake for 30 minutes, or until a knife inserted into the center comes out clean. Serve the pie warm or at room temperature.

Makes one 9-inch pie

Pie Pastry

Marion Harland's "cardinal motto for pastry-makers" in her 1871 book, *Common Sense in the Household*, was "Keep cool . . . . It is harder to make good pastry in warm weather than cold, on account of the tendency of the butter to oil, and thus render the crust heavy and solid." This advice still holds, although it is certainly easier to follow today with the help of refrigeration and air-conditioning.

1¼ cups flour
¾ teaspoon salt
4 tablespoons chilled butter, cut into pieces

3 tablespoons chilled vegetable shortening,
cut into pieces
4 to 5 tablespoons ice water

1. In a large bowl, combine the flour and salt. With a pastry blender or two knives, cut in the butter and shortening until the mixture resembles coarse crumbs.

2. Sprinkle 2 tablespoons of the ice water over the mixture and toss it with a fork. The dough should be just barely moistened, enough so it will hold together when it is formed into a ball. If necessary, add up to 3 tablespoons more water, 1 tablespoon at a time. Form the dough into a flat disk, wrap in plastic wrap, and refrigerate for at least 30 minutes.

3. On a lightly floured surface, roll the dough out to a 12-inch circle. Fit the dough into a 9-inch glass pie plate. Trim the overhang to an even ½ inch all the way around. Fold the overhang under and crimp the dough to form a decorative border. Prick the pastry with a fork. Place the pie shell in the freezer to chill for at least 15 minutes before baking. *Makes one 9-inch crust*

Shoofly Pie

To make this warmly spiced Pennsylvania-German specialty, you first prepare a rich butter crumble: part of it will be used in the filling, while the remainder will be needed for the crusty topping. This variation, with its moist filling, is referred to as a "wet" shoofly pie; so-called "dry" versions have a more cakelike texture, and are suitable for dunking. Both types demand strong, hot coffee as an accompaniment.

Pie Pastry (opposite)	3 tablespoons chilled butter, cut into pieces
1 cup flour	1 egg
½ cup to 1 cup (packed) brown sugar	¾ cup light unsulphured molasses
½ teaspoon cinnamon	1 cup boiling water
½ teaspoon nutmeg	1 teaspoon baking soda

1. Make the Pie Pastry.

2. Preheat the oven to 450°.

3. In a large bowl, combine the flour, sugar, cinnamon, and nutmeg. With a pastry blender or two knives, cut in the butter until the mixture resembles coarse crumbs. (Don't worry if the dry ingredients do not appear to be completely incorporated at this stage.)

4. In a medium bowl, lightly beat the egg. Beat in the molasses; set aside.

5. Pour the boiling water into a heatproof cup and stir in the baking soda. Gradually add the baking soda mixture to the molasses mixture, beating until well incorporated.

6. Remove the pie shell from the freezer. Stir 1 cup of the crumb mixture into the molasses mixture, and pour it into the pie shell. Sprinkle the remaining crumb mixture evenly over the filling and place the pie in the oven. Reduce the oven temperature to 350° and bake the pie for about 30 minutes, or until the filling is set and puffed, and does not quiver when the pie is shaken gently. Serve the pie slightly warm or at room temperature. *Makes one 9-inch pie*

Jefferson Davis Pie

Some recipes for Jefferson Davis pie contain a variety of spices. This version is flavored simply with vanilla and nutmeg; the taste is reminiscent of eggnog.

*S*cornful Yankees applied the name of Jefferson Davis, president of the Confederacy, to some Southern make-do foods necessitated by wartime shortages. For instance, "Jeff Davis coffee" was brewed from roasted grain. However, the origin of Jefferson Davis Pie has been traced to a cook whose master greatly admired the leader of the seceded states.

Pie Pastry (page 20)
¾ cup sugar
1 stick (4 ounces) butter, softened to
   room temperature
3 eggs

1 cup heavy cream
½ cup milk
2 tablespoons flour
1 teaspoon vanilla extract
½ teaspoon nutmeg

1. Make the Pie Pastry.
2. Preheat the oven to 400°.
3. Line the pie shell with foil, fill it with pie weights or dried beans, and bake it for 10 minutes. Remove the foil and weights, and set the pie shell aside to cool; reduce the oven temperature to 375°.
4. Make the filling: In a large bowl, cream the sugar and butter. Gradually beat in the eggs, cream, milk, flour, vanilla, and nutmeg. Pour the filling into the pie shell and bake for 20 minutes.
5. Reduce the oven temperature to 300° and bake for another 10 minutes, or until the filling is set and golden. Serve the pie warm or at room temperature.

Makes one 9-inch pie

Raisin-Currant Pie

Dried currants distinguish this attractive variation on the classic Pennsylvania-German raisin pie, a year-round favorite. If currants are not available, however, dark raisins would make an excellent substitute.

PASTRY
1¼ cups flour
¾ teaspoon salt
4 tablespoons chilled butter, cut into
   pieces
3 tablespoons chilled vegetable
   shortening, cut into pieces
¼ cup sour cream
1 to 2 tablespoons ice water
1 egg yolk beaten with 1 tablespoon milk

FILLING
2½ cups water
¼ cup flour
2 cups dried currants
1¼ cups golden raisins
¼ cup (packed) brown sugar
3 tablespoons lemon juice
1 tablespoon brandy
1 tablespoon butter
1 teaspoon grated lemon zest

1. Make the pastry: In a large bowl, combine the flour and salt. With a pastry blender or two knives, cut in the butter and shortening until the mixture resembles coarse crumbs. Add the sour cream and 1 tablespoon of the ice water, and toss the mixture with a fork. The dough should be just barely moistened, enough so it will hold

Raisin-Currant Pie

together when it is formed into a ball. If necessary, add up to 1 tablespoon more water. Form the dough into a flat disk, wrap in plastic wrap, and refrigerate for at least 30 minutes.

2. On a lightly floured surface, roll the dough out to a 12-inch circle. Fit the dough into a 9-inch glass pie plate. Trim the overhang to an even ½ inch all the way around. Fold the overhang under and crimp it to form a border. Prick the pastry with a fork. Place the pie shell in the freezer to chill for at least 15 minutes before baking.

3. Preheat the oven to 400°.

4. Line the pie shell with foil and fill it with pie weights or dried beans. Brush the pie border with the egg-yolk mixture and bake for 15 minutes. Remove the foil and weights, and set the pie shell aside to cool; reduce the oven temperature to 300°.

5. Make the filling: In a small bowl, stir together ¼ cup of the water and the flour; set aside. In a medium saucepan, combine the currants, raisins, and the remaining 2¼ cups water. Cook over medium heat, stirring often, until the mixture comes to a boil. Remove from the heat, add the flour mixture and sugar, and stir until well blended. Return the pan to the heat and cook, stirring often, until the mixture returns to a boil. Boil the mixture until it is slightly thickened, 1 to 2 minutes. Remove from the heat and blend in the lemon juice, brandy, butter, and lemon zest.

6. Pour the filling into the pie shell and spread it evenly with a spatula. Bake the pie for 30 minutes, or until the crust is lightly browned. Serve the pie warm.

Makes one 9-inch pie

Shaker-Style Lemon-Lime Pie

The Shakers enjoyed several types of lemon pie. In this recipe, lemon slices are macerated with sugar to soften the rinds enough so that the fruit is "candied" in the baking process. However, it is essential to use thin-skinned lemons. Weigh them in your hand before buying: thin-skinned lemons will seem heavy for their size.

3 thin-skinned lemons　　　　　　　　*Pie Pastry (page 20)*
Juice of 1 lime　　　　　　　　　　*1 egg yolk beaten with 1 tablespoon milk*
1½ cups sugar　　　　　　　　　　*5 eggs*

1. Scrub the lemons and cut them crosswise into paper-thin slices. Remove and discard the seeds and the pithy end slices. In a large bowl, combine the lemon slices, lime juice, and sugar. Toss well, cover with plastic wrap, and let stand at room temperature for at least 6 hours, or overnight. Stir the mixture occasionally.

2. Make the Pie Pastry. Preheat the oven to 400°.

3. Line the pie shell with foil, and fill it with pie weights or dried beans. Brush the crust with the egg-yolk mixture and bake for 10 minutes. Remove the foil and weights, and set the pie shell aside to cool; reduce the oven temperature to 350°.

4. In a large bowl, beat the eggs. Add the lemon mixture and stir gently. Pour the filling into the pie shell, distributing the lemon slices evenly, and bake for 35 to 40 minutes, or until the filling is puffed and golden.　　　　*Makes one 9-inch pie*

DECORATIVE PIE BORDERS

RIDGED FLUTE

A ridged flute is one of the easiest ways to dress up a pie. After trimming the overhang to an even ½ inch all around and turning it under, flute the dough by pinching it with the thumb and forefinger of one hand against the thumb of the other hand. Then, using your hand to support the flutes from underneath, press the tines of a fork into the pastry. This method should also flare the border out slightly without flattening it onto the rim of the pie plate.

AUTUMN LEAVES

Making a border of autumn leaves requires extra dough; see the pastry recipe for Sweet Potato Pie with Almond Topping (page 28) as a guide for quantities. Use two-thirds of the dough to line the pie plate, trim the overhang to an even ½ inch all around, and turn it under. Roll out the remaining dough to a thickness of about ⅛ inch and, with a knife, cut out leaf shapes of varying sizes. If desired, score vein patterns in the leaves with the tip of the knife. Pour the filling into the pie shell and then use egg yolk to attach the leaves to the edge of the pie. Let some of the leaves extend inward, beyond the pie edge and over the filling.

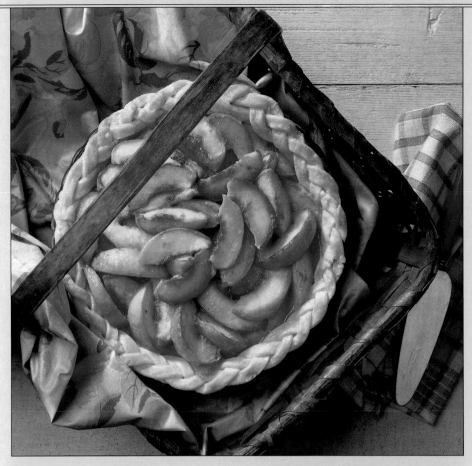

BRAIDED BORDER

A braided border adds a homey touch to any pie. Use a double-crust pastry recipe: half to line the pie plate and half for the braids. To make the braids, halve the reserved dough and roll out each half to a 20 x 1½-inch strip. Then, cut each strip into three smaller ½-inch-wide strips. Leaving the strips on the work surface, carefully braid each set. Brush the edge of the pie with egg glaze. Gently transfer the two braids to the pie and lightly press to secure them.

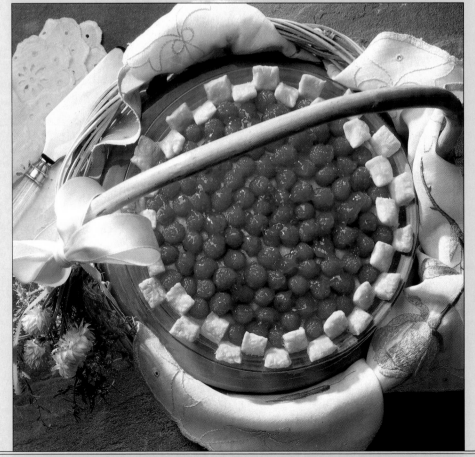

CASTLE TOP

Here is a marvelously simple but impressive treatment for a pie border. The castle top is suitable for a pie with a prebaked shell and an uncooked filling as well as for a pie whose filling and crust are baked together—the filling can help to support the border as it bakes. To make the border, use a single-crust pastry recipe to line the pie plate. Trim the overhang to an even ½ inch all around and turn it under; press lightly to seal and form a thick border. With a pair of kitchen scissors or a sharp knife, make cuts the full depth of the border, spaced about ¾ inch apart. Then fold in every other section of dough toward the center.

27

Sweet-Potato Pie with Almond Topping

Sweet potatoes are a Southern staple, and although pumpkin pies are also served in the South, sweet-potato-based desserts are more characteristic of the region. A rich, mellow flavor makes this pie a perfect conclusion to Thanksgiving dinner.

PASTRY
1¼ cups flour
½ cup yellow cornmeal
1 tablespoon granulated sugar
¾ teaspoon salt
6 tablespoons chilled butter, cut into pieces
4 tablespoons chilled vegetable
    shortening, cut into pieces
5 to 8 tablespoons ice water

FILLING
4 tablespoons butter, softened to room
    temperature
½ cup (packed) light brown sugar

2 large sweet potatoes, baked, peeled, and
    smoothly mashed (about 2 cups)
2 eggs, lightly beaten
½ cup heavy cream
1 tablespoon grated orange zest
½ teaspoon cinnamon

TOPPING AND GLAZE
¼ cup sliced almonds
1½ tablespoons flour
1½ tablespoons (packed) dark brown sugar
1 tablespoon chilled butter
1 egg yolk
1 tablespoon milk

1. Make the pastry: In a large bowl, combine the flour, cornmeal, granulated sugar, and salt. With a pastry blender or two knives, cut in the butter and shortening until the mixture resembles coarse crumbs.

2. Sprinkle 2 tablespoons of the ice water over the mixture and toss it with a fork. The dough should be just barely moistened, enough so it will hold together when it is formed into a ball. If necessary, add up to 6 tablespoons more water, 1 tablespoon at a time. Form the dough into a flat disk, wrap in plastic wrap, and refrigerate for at least 30 minutes. (If desired, use one-third of the dough to make a leaf border—see Decorative Pie Borders, pages 26-27.)

3. On a lightly floured surface, roll out the dough to a 12-inch circle. Fit the dough into a 9-inch glass pie plate. Trim the overhang to an even ½ inch all the way around. Fold the overhang under. Prick the bottom and sides of the pastry with a fork. Place the pie shell in the freezer to chill for at least 15 minutes before baking.

4. Make the filling: In a large bowl, cream the butter and light brown sugar until light and fluffy. Beat in the sweet potato until it is completely incorporated, then beat in the eggs. Add the cream, orange zest, and cinnamon, and continue beating until the mixture is smooth; set aside.

5. Preheat the oven to 350°.

6. Make the topping: Spread the almonds on a baking sheet and toast them in the oven, stirring occasionally, until golden, 5 to 10 minutes; set aside to cool briefly.

7. In a small bowl, combine the flour and dark brown sugar. Cut in the butter until the mixture resembles coarse crumbs. Stir in the almonds; set aside.

8. Make the egg glaze: In a small bowl, beat the egg yolk with the milk; set aside.

9. Spread the filling evenly in the pie shell, then sprinkle the topping over the

center of the filling. Brush the border of the crust with the egg glaze (if making the leaf border, use some of the egg-milk glaze to stick the leaves onto the pie border). Bake the pie for 30 to 35 minutes, or until the crust is golden. (If you have made the leaf border and it is browning too quickly, cover it with a crimped piece of foil.)

Makes one 9-inch pie

Osgood Pie

Osgood Pie (the name originally may have been "Oh So Good") belongs to the chess pie family. These pies, including pecan pie and Jefferson Davis Pie (page 22), have butter, eggs, and sugar (or molasses or syrup) as their basic filling ingredients. Stiffly beaten egg whites give Osgood Pie a light, cakelike texture, while nuts, fruit, and sweet spices impart a rich flavor reminiscent of fruitcake.

Pie Pastry (page 20)
1-cup chopped pecans
1 cup dried apricots, chopped
1 cup raisins
1 tablespoon flour
½ teaspoon allspice

½ teaspoon cinnamon
½ teapoon nutmeg
3 eggs, separated
½ cup sugar
2 tablespoons butter, melted
2 tablespoons cider vinegar

1. Make the Pie Pastry.

2. Preheat the oven to 400°.

3. Line the pie shell with foil, fill it with pie weights or dried beans, and bake it for 10 minutes. Remove the foil and weights and set the pie shell aside to cool; reduce the oven temperature to 375°.

4. Make the filling: In a large bowl combine the pecans, apricots, raisins, flour, allspice, cinnamon, and nutmeg, and toss to coat the nuts and fruit with the flour and spices; set aside.

5. Place the egg yolks in a large bowl. Gradually beat in the sugar and continue beating until the mixture is thick and light-colored. Add the butter and vinegar, and stir to blend. Stir in the nut and fruit mixture; set aside.

6. In another large bowl, beat the egg whites until stiff but not dry. Using a rubber spatula, gently fold the beaten whites into the nut and fruit mixture.

7. Spread the mixture evenly in the pie shell and bake for 18 to 20 minutes, or until the filling is set and golden, and a knife inserted into the center of the pie comes out clean. Serve warm.

Makes one 9-inch crust

Grasshopper Pie

Black Bottom Pie

The South takes credit for this recipe, which was a favorite of Floridian Marjorie Kinnan Rawlings, author of *Cross Creek Cookery* (and of *The Yearling*).

CHOCOLATE COOKIE CRUST
1 package (8½ ounces) chocolate wafers
⅓ cup butter, melted

FILLING AND TOPPING
3 ounces unsweetened chocolate
1 teaspoon vanilla extract
3 eggs, separated, plus 1 egg yolk
1 envelope unflavored gelatin

2 cups cold milk
2 tablespoons cornstarch
⅔ cup granulated sugar
¼ teaspoon salt
¼ teaspoon cream of tartar
2 tablespoons dark rum
Sweetened whipped cream and chocolate
  shavings, for garnish

   1. Make the crust: Place the wafers in a food processor or blender and process to form fine crumbs. Turn the crumbs into a bowl, add the melted butter, and blend well. Press the crumb mixture evenly into a 9-inch pie plate to form a crust; set aside.
   2. Make the filling: In the top of a double boiler over hot, not simmering, water, melt the chocolate. Remove the pan from the heat, stir in the vanilla, and set aside.
   3. In a small bowl, lightly beat the 4 egg yolks. In another small bowl, sprinkle the gelatin over ¼ cup of the milk. In a third small bowl, stir together the cornstarch and another ¼ cup of the milk. Set aside.

4. In a medium saucepan, scald the remaining 1½ cups milk. Stir ½ cup of the hot milk into the egg yolks; then stir in ⅓ cup of the granulated sugar, the cornstarch mixture, and the salt. Pour the egg-yolk mixture into the pan of hot milk and cook over medium heat, stirring constantly, until the custard is thick enough to coat the back of a spoon, 5 to 8 minutes. Stir in the gelatin mixture.

5. Divide the custard into two parts. Stir the chocolate mixture into one part, then immediately pour it into the crust. Set the remaining custard aside to cool.

6. In a large bowl, beat the egg whites until frothy. Add the cream of tartar and beat until soft peaks form. Gradually add the remaining ⅓ cup granulated sugar and continue beating until stiff peaks form.

7. Fold the beaten whites into the cooled custard, then gently stir in the rum. Spread the mixture carefully over the chocolate layer in the pie crust. Cover the pie with plastic wrap and refrigerate until well chilled and set, 3 to 4 hours.

8. Just before serving, top the pie with whipped cream and chocolate shavings.

Makes one 9-inch pie

Grasshopper Pie

Like the creamy cocktail for which it is named, Grasshopper Pie gets its vivid color from green crème de menthe, a mint-flavored liqueur. If crème de cacao (which is a chocolate-flavored liqueur) is not available, add a quarter-cup more crème de menthe.

Chocolate Cookie Crust (see Black Bottom
 Pie, opposite)
1 cup light cream or half-and-half
36 large marshmallows (4½ cups)
¼ cup green crème de menthe

¼ cup crème de cacao
2½ cups heavy cream
2 tablespoons confectioners' sugar
Chocolate shavings, for garnish (optional)

1. Follow Step 1 of the Black Bottom Pie recipe to make the Chocolate Cookie Crust; set aside.

2. In a medium saucepan, combine the light cream and marshmallows, and cook over medium heat, stirring constantly, until the marshmallows are completely melted, about 5 minutes. Remove the pan from the heat and stir in the crème de menthe and crème de cacao. Cover the pan and set the filling aside to cool to room temperature.

3. When the filling is cool, in a large bowl, beat 1½ cups of the heavy cream until stiff. Stir one-fourth of the whipped cream into the filling. Fold in the remaining whipped cream, then turn the filling into the crust, spreading it evenly with a rubber spatula. Place the pie in the freezer for at least 6 hours, or overnight.

4. Allow the pie to stand at room temperature for 15 minutes before serving.

5. Meanwhile, make the topping: Whip the remaining 1 cup heavy cream with the confectioners' sugar until stiff. Top the pie with the whipped cream and sprinkle with chocolate shavings, if desired.

Makes one 9-inch pie

Although chilled and frozen desserts have existed for centuries, they did not become generally popular until refrigerators were common in middle-class households. The recipe books that came with new refrigerators in the 1930s and '40s included instructions for Black Bottom Pie and for frozen desserts called "marlows," confected of marshmallows, whipped cream, and various flavorings.

Red, White, and Blue Pie

For many people, Independence Day means a picnic, and no picnic is really a picnic without a pie. This glorious dessert makes the best of summer's berries, and carries out the patriotic color scheme as well. To simplify your picnic-day plans, bake the crust the night before, then fill and decorate the pie shortly before serving time.

PASTRY
1¼ cups flour
2 tablespoons granulated sugar
7 tablespoons chilled butter, cut into pieces
4 to 5 tablespoons ice water

FILLING AND TOPPING
5 cups strawberries (2 pints)

2½ cups blueberries (1 pint)
¼ cup lemon juice
3 tablespoons cold water
1 tablespoon arrowroot or cornstarch
¼ cup granulated sugar
½ cup heavy cream
1 tablespoon confectioners' sugar

1. Make the pastry: In a large bowl, combine the flour and granulated sugar. With a pastry blender or two knives, cut in the butter until the mixture resembles coarse crumbs.

2. Sprinkle 2 tablespoons of the ice water over the mixture and toss it with a fork. The dough should be just barely moistened, enough so it will hold together when it is formed into a ball. If necessary, add up to 3 tablespoons more water, 1 tablespoon at a time. Form the dough into a flat disk, wrap in plastic wrap, and refrigerate for at least 30 minutes.

3. On a lightly floured surface, roll the dough out to a 12-inch circle. Fit the dough into a 9-inch glass pie plate. Trim the overhang to an even ½ inch all the way around. Fold the overhang under and crimp the dough to form a decorative border. Prick the pastry with a fork. Place the pie shell in the freezer to chill for at least 15 minutes before baking.

4. Preheat the oven to 400°.

5. Line the pie shell with foil, fill it with pie weights or dried beans, and bake for 10 minutes. Remove the foil and weights, reduce the oven temperature to 375°, and bake for another 10 to 12 minutes, or until light golden. Set aside to cool.

6. Place 1 cup of the strawberries and ½ cup of the blueberries in a small saucepan and crush them with a fork. In a small bowl, stir together the lemon juice, water, and arrowroot until blended, then add this mixture to the crushed berries. Stir in the granulated sugar, and cook over medium heat, stirring constantly, for 5 minutes, or until the mixture thickens and becomes translucent. Cover the berry glaze with plastic wrap and set aside to cool completely.

7. Place the remaining 4 cups strawberries and 2 cups blueberries in a medium bowl, pour the cooled berry glaze over them, and toss gently to coat. Spoon the berry mixture into the pie shell and refrigerate the pie until serving time.

8. Just before serving, make the topping: In a medium bowl, whip the cream with the confectioners' sugar until stiff. Spoon or pipe the sweetened whipped cream decoratively on top of the pie.

Makes one 9-inch pie

Red, White, and Blue Pie

RUSTIC FRUIT PIES

Here is an easy way to give a country look to a double-crust pie. Instead of top and bottom crusts, a single large crust is used to enclose the filling in a rustic-looking bundle. This method is well suited to fruit pies, and works best with fruits that hold their shape, such as apples, nectarines, peaches, and plums. The method is comfortingly flexible: Precision in rolling out and trimming the crust is not necessary, and the pie need not be baked in a round pie plate. As long as it holds about 1½ quarts, you can use any shape baking dish you like. When using a square-cornered dish, however, you should trim some dough from the folds in the corners; otherwise, they will be too thick and may not fully bake.

A. Roll the dough out to a 15-inch circle. Keep the rolling pin and the work surface lightly floured to avoid sticking.

B. Fit the dough into the baking dish, letting the edges hang over evenly all the way around. Spoon in the filling.

C. Bring the edges of the dough up over the filling, leaving an opening in the center. Brush with the egg glaze.

APPLE PIE WITH CHEDDAR CRUST

PASTRY
2¼ cups flour
½ teaspoon salt
10 tablespoons chilled butter, cut
    into pieces
1 cup grated Cheddar cheese
    (about ¼ pound)
5 to 6 tablespoons ice water

FILLING
3 medium Granny Smith apples,
    unpeeled and cubed (about 3
    cups)

1 tablespoon apple cider vinegar
¾ cup fresh breadcrumbs
⅓ cup (packed) light or dark
    brown sugar
½ cup finely chopped walnuts
¼ cup golden raisins
¼ teaspoon cinnamon
¼ teaspoon nutmeg
1 tablespoon butter

EGG GLAZE
1 egg yolk beaten with 1
    tablespoon milk

1. Make the pastry: In a large bowl, combine the flour and salt. With a pastry blender or two knives, cut in the chilled butter until the mixture resembles coarse crumbs. Stir in the grated cheese. Sprinkle 4 tablespoons of the ice water over the mixture and toss it with a fork. The dough should be just barely moistened, enough so it will hold together when it is formed into a ball. If necessary, add up to 2 tablespoons more water. Form the dough into a disk, wrap in plastic wrap, and refrigerate for at least 30 minutes.

2. Make the filling: Place the apples in a large bowl and sprinkle them with the vinegar. In a medium bowl, combine the breadcrumbs, sugar, walnuts, raisins, cinnamon, and nutmeg, and stir with a fork to mix well. Add the breadcrumb mixture to the apples and toss until they are well combined.

3. Preheat the oven to 425°.

4. On a lightly floured surface, roll the dough out to a 15-inch circle (Illustration A).

5. Line a 1½-quart deep-dish pie plate with the dough, letting the extra dough hang over the edges. Spoon the filling into the pie shell, mounding it slightly in the center (Illustration B). Dot the filling with the butter.

6. Gather up the dough overhang and fold it over the filling, leaving a 3- to 4-inch opening in the center (Illustration C). Brush the pie crust with the glaze and bake for 25 to 30 minutes, or until the crust is golden.

Makes one 9-inch pie

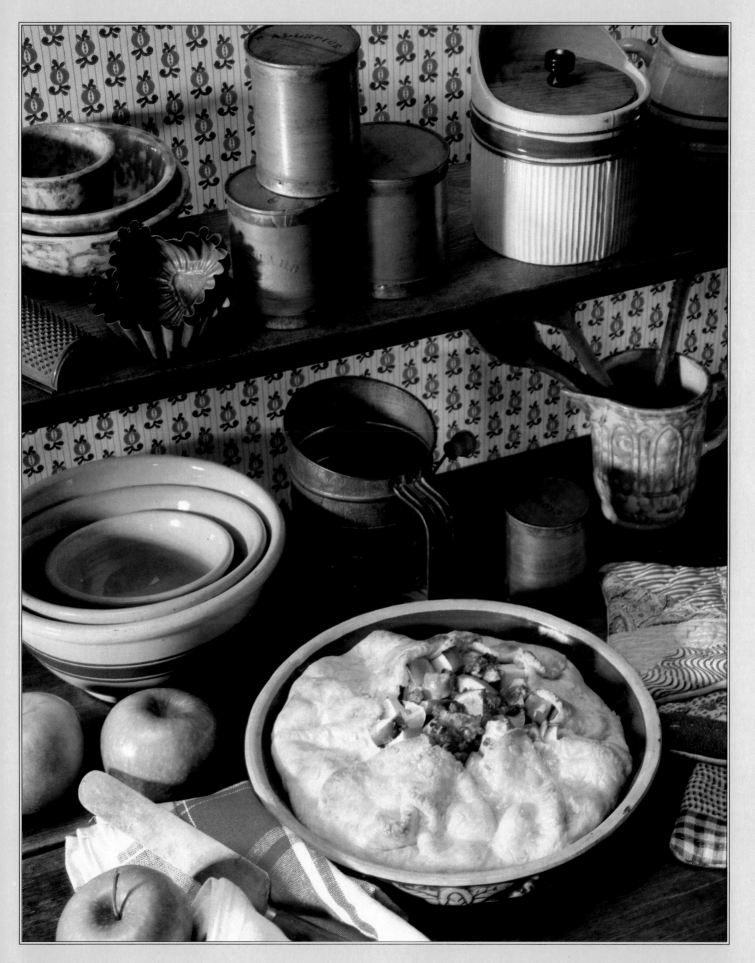

Banana-Strawberry Cream Pie

Banana cream pie is an American classic, but its smooth sweetness can be somewhat boring. Layering some fresh strawberries with the custard, bananas, and whipped cream adds a new spark to this family favorite. The ground toasted almonds in the crust add further variety of texture and flavor.

PASTRY
½ cup slivered blanched almonds
1⅓ cups flour
1 tablespoon granulated sugar
½ teaspoon salt
4 tablespoons chilled butter, cut into pieces
3 tablespoons chilled vegetable
    shortening, cut into pieces
4 to 5 tablespoons ice water

FILLING AND TOPPING
¼ cup flour

⅓ cup granulated sugar
3 egg yolks
1½ cups milk
1 tablespoon butter
1 teaspoon vanilla extract
4 ripe bananas
3 tablespoons lemon juice
2 cups strawberries
1 cup heavy cream
2 tablespoons confectioners' sugar

1. Preheat the oven to 375°.

2. Make the pastry: Spread the almonds in a shallow baking pan and toast them in the oven, stirring occasionally, for 5 minutes, or until golden. Turn off the oven. Transfer the almonds to a food processor and process just until finely ground, about 30 seconds; do not overprocess or the almonds will turn into an oily paste.

3. In a large bowl, combine the ground almonds, flour, granulated sugar, and salt. With a pastry blender or two knives, cut in the butter and shortening until the mixture resembles coarse crumbs.

4. Sprinkle 2 tablespoons of the ice water over the mixture and toss it with a fork. The dough should be just barely moistened, enough so it will hold together when it is formed into a ball. If necessary, add up to 3 tablespoons more water, 1 tablespoon at a time. Form the dough into a flat disk, wrap in plastic wrap, and refrigerate for at least 30 minutes.

5. On a lightly floured surface, roll the dough out to a 12-inch circle. Fit the dough into a 9-inch glass pie plate. Trim the overhang to an even ½ inch all the way around. Fold the overhang under and crimp the dough to form a decorative border. Prick the pastry with a fork. Place the pie shell in the freezer to chill for at least 15 minutes before baking.

6. Preheat the oven to 375°.

7. Line the pie shell with foil, fill it with pie weights or dried beans, and bake it for 10 minutes. Remove the foil and weights, and bake the pie shell for another 7 minutes, or until golden. Remove the pie shell from the oven and set it aside to cool.

8. Make the filling: In a medium saucepan, combine the flour and granulated sugar. Beat in the egg yolks, one at a time, then gradually add the milk, whisking constantly. Place the pan over medium heat. When the mixture has almost come to a

boil, reduce the heat to low and simmer, stirring constantly, until it is thick and custardy. Stir in the butter and vanilla, remove the pan from the heat, and set the filling aside to cool. Place a circle of waxed paper directly on the surface of the custard to prevent a skin from forming.

9. Slice the bananas ¼ inch thick and place them in a bowl. Sprinkle the lemon juice over them and toss to coat. Halve any large strawberries.

10. Spread half of the custard evenly in the pie shell, and arrange a layer of bananas and strawberries on top. Top with the remaining custard, bananas, and strawberries. Refrigerate the pie for at least 1 hour.

11. Before serving, make the topping: In a medium bowl, whip the cream with the confectioners' sugar until stiff. Spoon the whipped cream on top of the pie.

Makes one 9-inch pie

Tyler Pudding Pie

President John Tyler is one of several American political luminaries and military heroes to have had desserts named in their honor: Lafayette Gingerbread and Robert E. Lee Cake are two other examples. Virginia-born Tyler's name was given to this creation, which is buttery and caramel-flavored but not excessively sweet. It is said to have been served often at the White House during the Tyler administration.

Pie Pastry (page 20), made with
7 tablespoons of butter (omit the
vegetable shortening)

FILLING
2 eggs plus 2 egg yolks

1 cup (packed) brown sugar
1 stick (4 ounces) butter
½ cup heavy cream
½ teaspoon vanilla extract
¼ teaspoon nutmeg

1. Make the all-butter Pie Pastry; reserve the scraps.

2. Preheat the oven to 400°.

3. Line the pie shell with foil, fill it with pie weights or dried beans, and bake it for 10 minutes. Meanwhile, roll out the scraps of dough and cut out small stars or other decorative shapes; set aside. Remove the foil and weights from the pie shell and set it aside to cool; reduce the oven temperature to 375°.

4. Make the filling: In a medium bowl, beat the eggs and egg yolks until pale; set aside.

5. In a medium saucepan, combine the sugar, butter, and cream. Cook over medium heat, stirring constantly, until the sugar has dissolved and the butter is melted, 5 to 7 minutes.

6. Remove the pan from the heat and slowly add the beaten eggs, beating constantly. Stir in the vanilla and nutmeg, then pour the filling into the pie shell.

7. Arrange the pastry cutouts on top of the filling and bake for 20 minutes, or until the filling is puffed and rippled. Serve the pie warm.

Makes one 9-inch pie

FRIED PIES

Known variously as half-moon pies, mule ears, or crab lanterns—because of their semicircular shape—fried pies are usually associated with the South, although there are parts of New England that also lay claim to them.

These diminutive, deep-fried turnovers (small disks of dough folded over a fruit filling) are homey and satisfying. Not only are fried pies delightful for breakfast, afternoon snacks, or dessert, but, like other pastry-wrapped foods, they are eminently portable, making them perfect for lunchboxes, picnics, and other "fingerfood" situations. In fact, such pies were sometimes brought to church to keep restless children quiet, giving rise to yet another name, "preaching pies."

Traditionally, fried pies were filled with dried fruit; dried peaches, in particular, defined the Southern fried pie. Dried apples were also popular, and in New England, fried pies were often filled with applesauce. The use of dried fruits was motivated by practical, as much as gustatory, considerations, since fresh fruit was not available during the winter. A housewife's treasured stock of dried fruit was often the product of peach or apple bees, where women gathered to peel, slice, and dry fruit after the harvest.

Recipes for fried pies vary. Most call for a sturdy pie dough made with less fat than usual; but there are recipes that use biscuit or doughtnut dough. The fruit for the filling can be puréed or simply cooked until softened; and the amount of sugar and the kinds of spices used in a fried pie remain at the whim of the cook.

Buttermilk-Lemon Pie

Traditionally, this dessert was made in the winter, when the fresh fruit needed for pie fillings was unavailable. Pantries, however, were always stocked with flour, butter, eggs, milk, and sugar; vinegar could be used if there were no lemons on hand. This pie is unusual in that its thick custard filling, when baked, separates into two layers. The top is firm and rather cakelike; the bottom is soft and custardy.

PASTRY
1¼ cups flour
¾ teaspoon salt
7 tablespoons chilled butter, cut into pieces
3 tablespoons buttermilk
2 to 3 tablespoons ice water

FILLING
1 stick (4 ounces) butter, softened to
    room temperature

¾ cup sugar
3 eggs plus 2 egg yolks
¼ cup flour
1 cup buttermilk
1 tablespoon lemon juice
1 tablespoon grated lemon zest
1 teaspoon vanilla extract
½ teaspoon nutmeg

1. In a large bowl, combine the flour and salt. With a pastry blender or two knives, cut in the butter until the mixture resembles coarse crumbs.

2. Sprinkle the buttermilk and 1 tablespoon of ice water over the mixture and toss it with a fork. The dough should be just barely moistened, enough so it will hold together when it is formed into a ball. If necessary, add up to 2 tablespoons more water, 1 tablespoon at a time. Form the dough into a flat disk, wrap in plastic wrap, and refrigerate for at least 30 minutes.

3. On a lightly floured surface, roll the dough out to a 12-inch circle. Fit the dough into a 9-inch glass pie plate. Trim the overhang to an even ½ inch all the way around. Fold the overhang under and crimp the dough to form a decorative border. Prick the pastry with a fork. Place the pie shell in the freezer to chill for at least 15 minutes before baking.

4. Preheat the oven to 400°.

5. Line the pie shell with foil, fill it with pie weights or dried beans, and bake it for 10 minutes. Remove the foil and weights, and set the pie shell aside to cool; reduce the oven temperature to 350°.

6. Make the filling: In a large bowl, cream the butter and sugar until light and fluffy. Beat in the eggs and yolks one at a time, beating well after each addition. Beat in the flour. Still beating, slowly pour in the buttermilk, then stir in the lemon juice, zest, vanilla, and nutmeg.

7. Pour the filling into the pie shell and bake for 25 to 30 minutes, or until the filling is firm and golden. Cool the pie to room temperature before serving.

Makes one 9-inch pie

Blueberry Pie with Marmalade

Blueberry pie can be made throughout the year as long as the berries are frozen properly when they are in season. Dry-freezing works best: Spread the unwashed berries on sheets of foil, freeze them until they are rock-hard, and then seal them in plastic bags or freezer containers. Do not thaw the berries before using. Just rinse them briefly in cold water and drain them very thoroughly on paper towels.

The development of cultivated blueberries— the big, plump berries found in markets today—can be credited mainly to Elizabeth White of Whitesbog, in New Jersey's Pine Barrens. Working with agriculturist Dr. Frederick Coville, she crossbred native wild berry bushes and made the first commercial shipments of hybrid blueberries in 1916. Southern New Jersey is still a major blueberry growing area today.

PASTRY

1¼ cups flour

¼ cup yellow cornmeal

2 tablespoons sugar

1 teaspoon salt

6 tablespoons chilled butter, cut into pieces

4 tablespoons chilled vegetable
    shortening, cut into pieces

5 to 8 tablespoons ice water

FILLING AND GLAZE

5 cups blueberries (2 pints)

2 tablespoons lemon juice

¼ cup flour

2 tablespoons yellow cornmeal

⅓ cup orange marmalade

1 egg yolk

1 tablespoon milk

1. In a large bowl, combine the flour, cornmeal, sugar, and salt. With a pastry blender or two knives, cut in the butter and shortening until the mixture resembles coarse crumbs.

2. Sprinkle 2 tablespoons of the ice water over the mixture and toss it with a fork. The dough should be just barely moistened, enough so it will hold together when it is formed into a ball. If necessary, add up to 6 tablespoons more water, 1 tablespoon at a time. Separate one-third of the dough. Form both portions of dough into flat disks, wrap in plastic wrap, and refrigerate for at least 30 minutes.

3. On a lightly floured surface, roll out the larger portion of dough to a 12-inch circle. Fit the dough into a 9-inch glass pie plate. Trim the overhang to an even ½ inch all the way around. Fold the overhang under and score the edge of the crust with the pastry cutter to form a decorative border. Prick the pastry with a fork. Place the pie shell in the freezer to chill for at least 15 minutes before baking.

4. Meanwhile, roll out the remaining dough to a rough 9-inch square, then cut it into about twelve ½-inch-wide strips. Working on a baking sheet lined with waxed paper, weave the strips of dough into a lattice. Place the lattice, still on the waxed paper, in the freezer to chill.

5. Preheat the oven to 375°.

6. Make the filling and glaze: Place the blueberries in a large bowl, sprinkle them with the lemon juice, and toss gently. In a small bowl, stir together the flour, cornmeal, and marmalade, then stir the mixture into the berries; set aside. In a small bowl, stir together the egg yolk and milk.

7. Pour the berry filling into the pie shell. Carefully place the lattice on top of the filling and trim the ends of the lattice strips even with the rim of the crust. Brush the rim and lattice with the egg glaze, and bake for 20 to 25 minutes, or until the crust is golden. Serve the pie warm or at room temperature. *Makes one 9-inch pie*

Coconut Cream Pie with Chocolate-Coconut Crust

This no-bake pie (except for toasting the coconut) is perfect for hot-weather entertaining, but its delightful flavor justifies serving it through the year. Toasted coconut enhances the pie in a number of ways: Some of it is mixed with melted chocolate to form a crunchy crust; a generous amount is blended into the rich custard filling to give it a nut-like flavor; and the remaining portion is sprinkled over dollops of whipped cream to make an attractive topping.

1 package (7 ounces) sweetened shredded coconut (about 3 cups)
3 ounces semisweet chocolate
2 tablespoons butter
⅓ cup granulated sugar
¼ cup cornstarch

4 egg yolks
2 cups milk
½ teaspoon coconut extract
½ cup heavy cream
2 tablespoons confectioners' sugar

1. Preheat the oven to 325°.

2. Spread the coconut in a large, shallow baking pan and toast it in the oven, stirring occasionally, until lightly browned, about 10 minutes.

3. Meanwhile, in the top of a double boiler over hot, not simmering, water, melt the chocolate and butter. Remove the pan from the heat and stir 2 cups of the toasted coconut into the chocolate mixture.

4. Turn the coconut-chocolate mixture into a 9-inch pie plate and pat it evenly into the plate to form a crust. Cover the crust with plastic wrap and refrigerate it for at least 15 minutes, or until firm.

5. Meanwhile, make the filling: In a medium saucepan, combine the granulated sugar and cornstarch. Gradually whisk in the egg yolks, then slowly add the milk, whisking constantly, until the mixture is smooth and the sugar is dissolved. Place the pan over medium heat, and cook the mixture, whisking constantly, until it is thick enough to coat the back of a spoon, 5 to 10 minutes.

6. Stir in the coconut extract and ¾ cup of the remaining toasted coconut. Let the filling cool slightly, then place a circle of waxed paper directly on the surface of the custard to prevent a skin from forming. Place the filling in the refrigerator to chill for at least one hour.

7. Just before serving, make the whipped cream topping: In a medium bowl, whip the cream with the confectioners' sugar until stiff.

8. Spoon the filling into the crust. Top the pie with the whipped cream, then sprinkle with the remaining ¼ cup coconut.   *Makes one 9-inch pie*

Lemon-Orange Meringue Pie

Under its lofty topping, this pie conceals a flavor twist—a hint of orange in the classic lemon filling. A golden meringue-crowned pie is a proud achievement for any baker, and despite its impressive appearance, it isn't really a difficult dessert to prepare. One basic rule to follow: When spooning the meringue over the filling, be sure to spread it evenly to the edges so that the topping touches the crust all the way around. This will help prevent the meringue from shrinking as it bakes.

Pie Pastry (page 20)
¾ cup plus ⅓ cup sugar
¼ cup cornstarch
3 tablespoons flour
1¾ cups milk
4 eggs, separated

⅓ cup lemon juice
2 tablespoons butter, cut into pieces
1 tablespoon grated lemon zest
1 tablespoon grated orange zest
1 teaspoon orange extract
¼ teaspoon cream of tartar

1. Make the Pie Pastry.

2. Preheat the oven to 400°.

3. Line the pie shell with foil, fill it with pie weights or dried beans, and bake it for 10 minutes. Remove the foil and weights, and set the pie shell aside to cool; reduce the oven temperature to 350°.

4. Make the filling: In a medium saucepan, combine ¾ cup of the sugar, the cornstarch, and flour. Place the pan over medium heat and slowly add the milk, whisking constantly. Continue cooking and whisking until the mixture is thick enough to coat the back of a spoon. Remove the pan from the heat and let the mixture cool slightly.

5. Add the egg yolks, one at a time. Then add the lemon juice, and whisk until well blended. One ingredient at a time, add the butter, lemon and orange zests, and orange extract, whisking well after each addition; the custard should be very thick. Set the pan in a large bowl of cold water to cool for about 5 minutes.

6. Meanwhile, make the meringue: In a large bowl, beat the egg whites until frothy. Add the cream of tartar and continue beating until soft peaks form. Gradually add the remaining ⅓ cup sugar and continue beating until stiff, glossy peaks form.

7. Turn the cooled filling into the pie shell, spreading it evenly with a rubber spatula. Spoon the meringue on top, mounding it into peaks and being careful to have it meet the crust at the edges. Bake for 8 to 10 minutes, or until the meringue is lightly browned. Serve the pie slightly warm, or at room temperature.

Makes one 9-inch pie

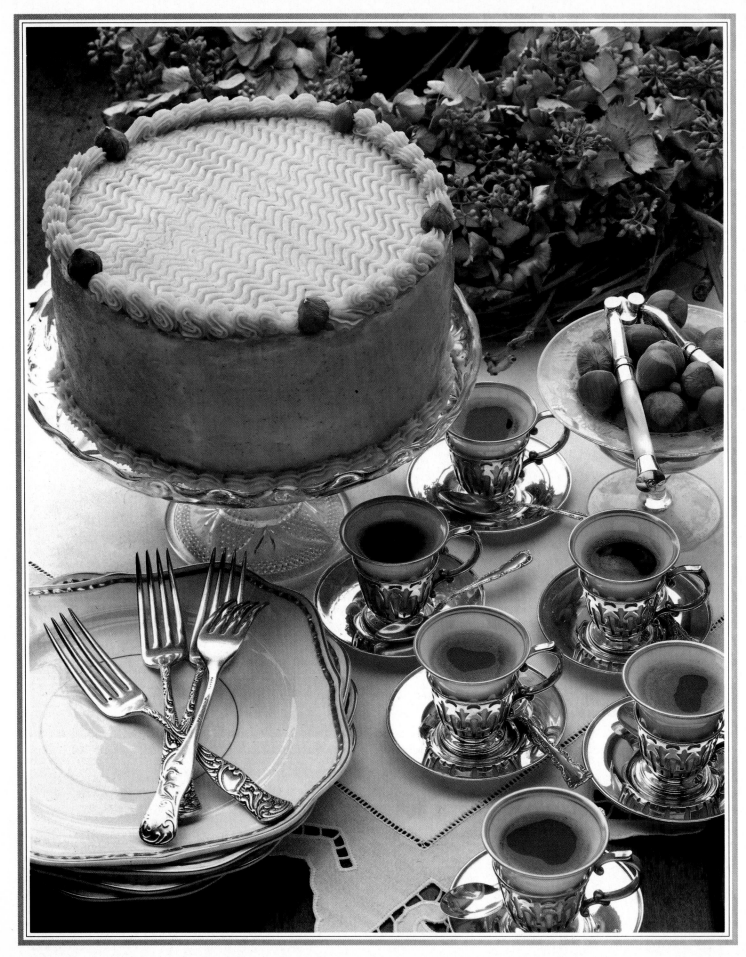

Cakes

crowning creations made with
country-fresh ingredients

Mary Randolph's 1824 fruitcake recipe required a wealth of ingredients, not to mention time and energy: "Four pounds of flour dried and sifted; four pounds of butter washed to free it from salt; two pounds of loaf sugar pounded . . . wash four pounds of currants clean, pick and dry them . . . stone two pounds of raisins." This was all preparatory to beating thirty egg whites to a "froth"—by hand, of course. Today, scratch cakes still require quality ingredients and a bit of time, but compared to quick-mix products, they are well worth the effort.

Whether beaten by hand in an old yellow batter bowl or whipped up in a modern mixing machine, a perfect cake is a triumph for any cook. Who does not remember making a lofty layer cake for the first time and proudly presenting it at the family table? The recipes in this chapter will expand your repertoire. Try a lemon cake roll for an afternoon tea or serve a berry-filled ice cream cake on a hot summer day. And, for those times when all you've got on hand is butter, sugar, flour, and eggs, there is the simple 1-2-3-4 Cake, a classic recipe that never fails.

Filbert Cake with Coffee Buttercream makes a fine finale to an elegant dinner.

Lemon Cake Roll

Rolled cakes, such as jelly rolls, are usually sponge cakes—or "collapsed" soufflés —baked in shallow pans and then rolled up around a filling of jelly, jam, or whipped cream. This one is filled with lemon curd, a thick custard traditionally used as a filling for tarts or a spread for toast. If the cake is served soon after it is assembled, the lemon curd will be soft and creamy. However, if the cake is refrigerated for several hours before it is to be eaten, the filling will be firmer and thicker.

Although a turn-of-the-century cookbook suggested the following method for saving eggs, it seems rather strange advice today: "Stir your cakes the same as usual except that you leave out the eggs. After your baking powder is added and tins greased, the very last thing before placing them in the oven, stir in one tablespoon of clear snow for each egg you would have used. Your cakes will be light and tender."

CAKE
½ cup sifted cake flour
¼ teaspoon baking powder
¼ teaspoon salt
4 eggs, separated
1 teaspoon grated lemon zest
¼ teaspoon lemon extract
¼ teaspoon cream of tartar
½ cup granulated sugar
2 tablespoons confectioners' sugar

LEMON-CURD FILLING
8 egg yolks
1 stick (4 ounces) butter
⅔ cup granulated sugar
½ cup lemon juice, preferably fresh
2 teaspoons grated lemon zest

GARNISH
2 tablespoons confectioners' sugar

1. Preheat the oven to 400°. Butter the bottom of a 15½ x 10½-inch jelly roll pan and line the bottom with waxed paper. Butter and flour the waxed paper.

2. Make the cake: In a medium bowl, stir together the cake flour, baking powder, and salt.

3. In a small bowl, beat together the 4 egg yolks, lemon zest, and lemon extract. Stir in half of the dry ingredients.

4. In a large bowl, beat the egg whites until frothy. Add the cream of tartar and continue beating until soft peaks form. Gradually add the granulated sugar and continue beating until stiff, glossy peaks form.

5. Fold one-fourth of the beaten egg whites into the egg-yolk mixture, then fold in the remaining egg whites. Sprinkle the remaining dry ingredients over the egg mixture and gently fold them in until no streaks remain. Immediately spread the batter evenly in the prepared pan. Bake for 8 to 10 minutes, or until the top of the cake springs back when touched with your finger and a toothpick inserted in the center of the cake comes out clean and dry.

6. Lay a kitchen towel on a work surface and sift the 2 tablespoons of confectioners' sugar over it. Run a knife around the edge of the pan to loosen the cake, then turn the cake out onto the towel. Carefully peel off the waxed paper, using a sharp knife to free it if it sticks.

7. If the edges of the cake are crisp or browned, carefully trim them. Starting with one short side, roll the cake and towel together into a log. Set the wrapped cake aside to cool to room temperature before filling.

8. Meanwhile, make the lemon-curd filling: In a small bowl, beat the 8 egg yolks until pale and lemon-colored; set aside.

9. In a small, heavy saucepan, melt the butter over medium heat. Add the

Lemon Cake Roll

granulated sugar, lemon juice and zest, and stir until well combined. Drizzle a little of the warm butter mixture into the beaten egg yolks, stirring constantly, then beat the egg-yolk mixture into the butter mixture. Cook, stirring constantly, until the mixture has thickened and is almost boiling, about 6 minutes; be careful not to let the mixture come to a boil.

10. Remove the pan from the heat and let the lemon curd cool slightly, then cover it with waxed paper and let it cool completely, stirring occasionally; it will thicken further as it cools. Refrigerate the lemon curd until ready to assemble the cake.

11. Assemble the cake: Gently unroll the cake; do not attempt to flatten it completely. Spread the cooled lemon curd evenly over the cake to within 1 inch of the edges. Starting with one short side, reroll the cake, finishing with the seam side down. Using two metal spatulas, transfer the cake to a serving platter. If not serving the cake immediately, cover it with plastic wrap and refrigerate.

12. If desired, for a neater presentation, trim a thin slice from each end of the cake roll to even it.

13. Just before serving, sift the confectioners' sugar over the cake.

Makes one 10-inch cake roll

Filbert Cake with Coffee Buttercream

In America, filberts, or hazelnuts, are grown mainly in the Pacific Northwest. Among the sweetest of nuts, they have long been recognized as a toothsome complement to chocolate. In this recipe, their delicious flavor blends particularly well with the coffee-flavored buttercream frosting. Be sure to use powdered instant coffee for the buttercream; instant coffee crystals may not dissolve completely.

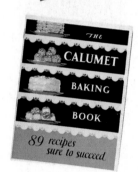

CAKE
1 cup shelled filberts
2¾ cups sifted cake flour
2 teaspoons baking powder
¼ teaspoon salt
2 sticks (8 ounces) butter, softened to
  room temperature
1½ cups sugar
3 eggs
1 cup sour cream
1 teaspoon vanilla extract

COFFEE BUTTERCREAM
¾ cup sugar
⅓ cup water
⅛ teaspoon cream of tartar
4 egg yolks
3 sticks (12 ounces) butter, softened to
  room temperature and cut into
  1-tablespoon pieces
2 teaspoons instant coffee powder,
  preferably espresso
1 teaspoon vanilla extract

1. Make the cake: Preheat the oven to 375°. Butter the bottoms of two 8-inch round cake pans, then line them with circles of waxed paper. Butter and flour the waxed paper.

2. Place the filberts in a shallow baking pan and toast in the oven, stirring occasionally, until slightly browned, 5 to 10 minutes. Set aside to cool slightly. Reduce the oven temperature to 350°. Set aside 5 filberts for the garnish, and process the remaining filberts in a food processor just until finely ground; do not overprocess or the nuts will turn into a paste. Set aside.

3. In a medium bowl, stir together the flour, baking powder, and salt.

4. In a large bowl, cream the butter and sugar. Beat in the eggs, one at a time, beating well after each addition, then beat in the sour cream and vanilla. Gradually add the dry ingredients, beating well after each addition. Beat in the ground filberts.

5. Spread the batter evenly in the prepared pans. Rap the pans once or twice on the counter to remove any air pockets. Bake for 30 to 35 minutes, or until the cakes shrink from the sides of the pans and a toothpick inserted in the center of each cake comes out clean and dry. Let the cakes cool in the pans for 10 minutes, then turn them out onto racks to cool completely before frosting.

6. Meanwhile, make the buttercream: In a small, heavy saucepan, bring the sugar, water, and cream of tartar to a boil over medium-high heat. Reduce the heat to medium so that the mixture simmers, and cook, without stirring, until the sugar syrup registers exactly 238° on a candy thermometer, about 20 minutes.

7. In a medium bowl, beat the egg yolks until pale and lemon-colored. Slowly drizzle in the hot sugar syrup and beat constantly until cool, about 10 minutes.

8. Gradually beat in the butter, then the instant coffee and vanilla. Continue beating until the buttercream is uniform in color and just spreadable, about 3 minutes.

9. Assemble the cake: Remove the waxed paper from the layers. Set aside 1 cup of the buttercream for decoration, then spread a generous layer of buttercream over one cake layer. Top with the second layer, then spread a thin coat of buttercream over the top and sides of the cake. Refrigerate the cake for about 15 minutes to set the frosting, then spread a ¼-inch-thick layer of buttercream over the first coat. Fill a pastry bag with the reserved buttercream and pipe it decoratively on the cake. Garnish with the reserved filberts.

Makes one 8-inch layer cake

White Fruitcake

Fruitcake baking was traditionally a large-scale operation. *The Carolina Housewife*, published in 1847, included a recipe requiring twenty pounds each of butter, sugar, flour, and raisins; forty pounds of currants; twenty nutmegs; and twenty glasses each of wine and brandy. This more manageable recipe for a white fruitcake, with mostly light-colored fruit, makes six small loaves, which are perfect for holiday gifts. Bake each one in a separate foil pan, then wrap individually in festive seasonal papers.

2 cups golden raisins	*2 sticks (8 ounces) butter*
1 cup chopped dried apricots	*1 cup sugar*
1 cup chopped mixed dried fruit	*8 eggs*
1 cup brandy	*2 cups slivered blanched almonds*
2 cups flour	*2 teaspoons grated lemon zest*
2 teaspoons baking powder	*2 teaspoons vanilla extract*
1 teaspoon salt	*6 tablespoons bourbon*

1. In a medium bowl, combine the raisins, apricots, and dried fruit, and pour the brandy over them. Set aside to soak for at least 4 hours, or overnight.

2. Preheat the oven to 325°. Butter six 5½ x 3 x 2-inch mini loaf pans.

3. In a small bowl, stir together the flour, baking powder, and salt; set aside.

4. In a large bowl, cream the butter and sugar. Beat in the eggs, one at a time. Alternating among the three, stir in the dry ingredients, the fruit-brandy mixture, and the almonds, beating well after each addition. Blend in the lemon zest and vanilla.

5. Divide the batter evenly among the prepared pans (they will be nearly full). Rap the pans once or twice on the counter to remove any air pockets. (For easier handling, place the pans on a large baking sheet.) Bake for 45 to 50 minutes, or until the cakes shrink from the sides of the pans and a toothpick inserted in the center of each cake comes out clean and dry.

6. Let the cakes cool in the pans on racks for 30 minutes, then turn them out to cool completely.

7. Pour 1 tablespoon of bourbon over each cake and let stand for at least 4 hours. If not serving immediately, wrap each cake in a bourbon-soaked cheesecloth, then in plastic wrap, and store in a tightly closed container for up to 3 months. The cakes may also be frozen for up to 4 months.

Makes 6 mini loaves

Pineapple-Coconut Upside-Down Cake

Although fresh pineapples were sold in Eastern and Southern seaport cities in the 18th and 19th centuries, the fruit was not very popular until canned pineapple was marketed, beginning around 1910. Recipes for pineapple upside-down cake began to appear at about the same time.

1 stick (4 ounces) butter, softened to
   room temperature
¾ cup (packed) dark brown sugar
1¼ cups sweetened shredded coconut
1 cup sliced almonds
10 juice-packed pineapple slices, drained
   (from a 20-ounce can)

1½ cups flour
1 teaspoon baking powder
¼ teaspoon salt
½ cup granulated sugar
1 teaspoon vanilla extract
2 eggs, lightly beaten
½ cup sour cream

1. Preheat the oven to 350°.

2. In a small, heavy saucepan, melt 4 tablespoons of the butter over medium heat. Add the brown sugar, and cook, stirring constantly, until the sugar dissolves and the mixture is thick and bubbly, about 2 minutes.

3. Carefully (the mixture will be extremely hot) pour the sugar mixture into an ungreased 9-inch round cake pan. Sprinkle the sugar mixture with ¼ cup of the coconut and ½ cup of the almonds, then quickly arrange the pineapple slices, over-lapping slightly, over the mixture, and press them down gently; set aside.

4. In a small bowl, stir together the flour, baking powder, and salt; set aside.

5. In a large bowl, cream the remaining 4 tablespoons butter with the granulated sugar. Beat in the vanilla, then the lightly beaten eggs, and continue beating until the mixture is light and fluffy.

6. Alternately add the dry ingredients, the sour cream, and the remaining 1 cup of coconut and ½ cup of almonds, beating well after each addition.

7. Spread the batter evenly over the pineapple layer. Rap the pan gently once or twice on the counter to remove any air pockets. Bake for 40 to 45 minutes, or until the cake shrinks from the sides of the pan and a toothpick inserted in the center of the cake comes out clean and dry.

8. Immediately run the tip of a knife around the edge of the pan to loosen the cake, then turn it out onto a plate. Serve the cake warm, or at room temperature.

Makes one 9-inch cake

Pineapple-Coconut Upside-Down Cake

Blackberry Jam Cake

Shelves stocked with an array of rainbow-colored preserves were once the pride of every conscientious country housewife, and jams and jellies were common ingredients in 19th-century cakes, used as flavorings, fillings, and frostings. Blackberry jam tints this cake a delicate, Victorian mauve color.

CAKE

2¼ cups flour

1 teaspoon baking soda

1 teaspoon cinnamon

½ teaspoon grated nutmeg

¼ teaspoon salt

1½ sticks (6 ounces) butter, softened to
    room temperature

1 cup sugar

3 eggs, separated

⅓ cup buttermilk or plain yogurt

1 cup blackberry jam

1 tablespoon grated orange zest

½ teaspoon orange extract

FROSTING

11 ounces cream cheese, softened to
    room temperature

1 stick (4 ounces) butter, softened to
    room temperature

2 teaspoons grated orange zest

1½ teaspoons vanilla extract

2 cups sifted confectioners' sugar

Fresh blackberries and strips of orange
    zest, for garnish (optional)

1. Make the cake: Preheat the oven to 350°. Butter two 8-inch round cake pans and line the bottoms with circles of waxed paper. Butter the waxed paper, then flour the pans.

2. In a small bowl, stir together the flour, baking soda, cinnamon, nutmeg, and salt. Set aside.

3. In a large bowl, cream the butter and sugar until light and fluffy; set aside. In a medium bowl, beat the egg yolks until pale and lemon-colored, then beat them into the butter-sugar mixture. Beat in the buttermilk, jam, orange zest and extract, then stir in the dry ingredients.

4. In a medium bowl, beat the egg whites until stiff but not dry. Gently fold one-fourth of the egg whites into the batter, then fold in the remaining egg whites.

5. Spread the batter evenly in the prepared pans. Rap the pans once or twice on the counter to remove any air pockets. Bake for 45 to 50 minutes, or until the cakes shrink from the sides of the pans and a toothpick inserted in the center of each cake comes out clean and dry. Let the cakes cool in the pans for 10 minutes, then turn them out onto racks to cool completely before and frosting.

6. Meanwhile, make the frosting: In a medium bowl, beat the cream cheese and butter until smooth. Beat in the orange zest and vanilla extract. Gradually add the confectioners' sugar, beating well until the frosting is thick and smooth.

7. Frost the cake: Remove the waxed paper from the layers. Spread a generous layer or frosting over one cake layer. Top with the second layer, then frost the top and sides of the cake. Decorate the cake with fresh blackberries and strips of orange zest, if desired.

Makes one 8-inch layer cake

Marble Spice Cake

Marble cakes used to be made by coloring and flavoring part of the batter with dark spices and molasses rather than chocolate. The marble swirls in this cake, however, taste of allspice and ginger as well as a delicate hint of chocolate.

SPICE CAKE BATTER

1 cup milk

1 tablespoon lemon juice

2 ounces semisweet chocolate

2 cups sifted cake flour

1 teaspoon baking soda

1 teaspoon allspice

1 teaspoon ground ginger

1 stick (4 ounces) butter, softened to
   room temperature

¾ cup (packed) dark brown sugar

4 egg yolks

⅓ cup molasses

WHITE CAKE BATTER

2½ cups sifted cake flour

2 teaspoons baking powder

1 stick (4 ounces) butter, softened to
   room temperature

¾ cup granulated sugar

¾ cup milk

1 teaspoon vanilla extract

1 cup finely chopped blanched almonds

4 egg whites

1. Preheat the oven to 350°. Generously butter and flour a 10-inch tube pan.

2. Make the spice cake batter: In a cup, stir together ¾ cup of the milk and the lemon juice; set aside.

3. In the top of a double boiler, over hot, not simmering, water, melt the chocolate in the remaining ¼ cup of milk, stirring until smooth. Set aside to cool.

4. In a medium bowl, stir together the flour, baking soda, allspice, and ginger.

5. In a large bowl, cream the butter and brown sugar until light and fluffy. Beat in the egg yolks, one at a time, then beat in the molasses and the chocolate mixture.

6. Alternating between the two, add the flour mixture and the lemon-milk mixture, beating well after each addition. Set the spice batter aside.

7. Make the white cake batter: In a medium bowl, stir together the flour and baking powder; set aside. In a large bowl, cream the butter and granulated sugar until light and fluffy. Alternating between the two, add the flour mixture and the milk, beating well after each addition. Stir in the vanilla and almonds; set aside.

8. In a large bowl, beat the egg whites until stiff peaks form. Gently fold the beaten egg whites into the white cake batter.

9. Using two ¼-cup measures, scoop a portion of each batter into the prepared pan. Alternate scoops of each batter to cover the bottom of the pan. Make a second layer of batter in the same fashion, placing dark batter on light and light on dark. Repeat until all the batter is used.

10. Rap the pan once or twice on the counter to remove any air pockets. Bake for 1 hour and 15 to 20 minutes, or until the cake shrinks from the sides of the pan and a toothpick inserted in the center of the cake comes out clean and dry. Let the cake cool in the pan for 10 minutes, then turn it out onto a cake rack to cool completely.

Makes one 10-inch tube cake

CANDIED FRUITS

Candying fruits is a time-honored way to preserve them, and the jewellike fruits make enchanting cake decorations. The recipes given here are for small, whole fruits, which can be used to create a colorful wreath. This project will reward you with a trove of candied fruits, which, if refrigerated, will keep for months. Be sure to use firm, sound fruits.

CRANBERRIES

Rinse, pick over, and drain 1 pound of cranberries; place in a heatproof bowl. In a small saucepan, bring 1½ cups of water and 2½ cups of sugar to a boil over medium heat, stirring to dissolve the sugar. Pour the boiling syrup over the berries. Place a rack over several inches of boiling water in a large saucepan. Place the bowl on the rack (the water should not touch the bottom of the bowl), cover the pan, and steam the cranberries, replenishing the water if necessary, for 45 minutes. Remove the bowl from the pan and let the cranberries cool in the syrup; do not stir them. Leave them at room temperature for several days, stirring occasionally. When the syrup is as thick as jelly, remove the cranberries and spread them out on waxed paper to dry for three days, or until they are no longer sticky. Store in an airtight container.

LADY APPLES

Wash 1 pound of lady apples. With a sharp knife, slit the skin of each apple from the stem to the blossom end. Place the apples in a heatproof bowl. In a small saucepan, bring 1½ cups of

water and 2½ cups of sugar to a boil, stirring to dissolve the sugar. Pour the boiling syrup over the apples. Steam the apples as directed for cranberries (at left). Cover the bowl and let the apples cool in the syrup overnight. Transfer the apples and syrup to a saucepan. Bring the syrup slowly to a boil, then simmer, uncovered, until the syrup registers 225° on a candy thermometer. Remove the pan from the heat, cover, and let the apples cool in the syrup. Store the apples in the syrup in jars.

KUMQUATS OR LIMEQUATS

Scrub 1 pound of kumquats or limequats in warm soapy water; rinse well. In a large covered saucepan, simmer the fruits in water to cover for 45 minutes. Meanwhile, in a medium saucepan, bring 6 cups of water and 2¼ cups of sugar to a boil, stirring to dissolve the sugar. Drain the fruits and return them to the pan. Add the syrup and simmer, uncovered, until the syrup has thickened slightly and registers 223° on a candy thermometer, and the fruits are translucent. Remove the pan from the heat, cover, and let the fruits cool in the syrup. Store the kumquats or limequats in their syrup in jars, or dry them on a rack for several days, then store them in airtight containers.

The cake at right is decorated with a wreath of homemade candied cranberries, lady apples, kumquats, and limequats, in addition to storebought seckel pears. Other candied fruits—such as the cherries, angelica, and citron shown here—are widely available in specialty food shops.

Berry-Orange Ice Cream Cake

Virtually any fruit-flavored ice cream, store-bought or homemade, can be used as a filling for this cake. Or, start with a pint of vanilla and stir in fresh or frozen blueberries, raspberries, blackberries, pitted sweet cherries, peaches, or nectarines (cut up or dice the larger berries and fruits). Just before serving, decorate the cake with fresh whole berries or slices of fruit.

1⅓ cups sifted cake flour	¼ teaspoon orange extract
¾ teaspoon baking powder	½ teaspoon cream of tartar
¼ teaspoon salt	1 pint strawberry ice cream
5 eggs, separated	½ pint heavy cream
1¼ cups granulated sugar	¼ cup sifted confectioners' sugar
3 tablespoons milk	Fresh strawberries, for garnish
2 teaspoons grated orange zest	

1. Make the cake: Preheat the oven to 350°. Butter a 13 x 9-inch cake pan and line the bottom with waxed paper. Butter the waxed paper, then flour the pan.

2. In a small bowl, stir together the flour, baking powder, and salt.

3. In a large bowl, beat the egg yolk and granulated sugar until the mixture is pale and lemon-colored. Add the milk, then beat in the orange zest and extract.

4. Gradually beat in the flour mixture, beating well after each addition.

5. In another large bowl, beat the egg whites until frothy. Add the cream of tartar and continue beating until stiff peaks form. Fold one-fourth of the beaten egg whites into the batter, then fold in the remaining egg whites.

6. Spread the batter evenly in the prepared pan. Rap the pan once or twice on the counter to remove any air pockets. Bake for 25 to 30 minutes, or until the cake shrinks from the sides of the pan and a toothpick inserted in the center of the cake comes out clean and dry. Let the cake cool in the pan for 10 minutes, then turn it out onto a rack to cool completely before assembling.

7. Set out the ice cream to soften at room temperature until just spreadable. Meanwhile, remove the waxed paper from the cake. Cut the cake in half lengthwise to form two 13 x 4½-inch layers. Place one layer of cake on a large sheet of foil.

8. Spread the ice cream over the bottom layer, then cover it with the second layer, pressing it down lightly. Wrap the cake in the foil and place it in the freezer until the ice cream is firm, at least 3 hours, or overnight.

9. Just before serving, trim the sides of the cake with a long, serrated knife to create a smooth surface. Transfer the cake to a serving platter. In a large bowl, whip the cream until soft peaks form. Gradually add the confectioners' sugar and continue whipping until the cream holds stiff peaks.

10. Reserve ¾ cup of whipped cream for decorating, then spread a thick layer of whipped cream over the top and sides of the cake. Pipe the reserved whipped cream decoratively around the edges of the cake, and garnish with whole strawberries. If not serving immediately, return the cake to the freezer.

Makes one 13-inch loaf cake

A 1916 book of household hints suggested the following "Improvised Cake-mixer" as a time- and labor-saving device: "By putting the ingredients into a two-quart ice cream freezer you can beat them quickly and easily, the result being cakes of very fine grain. The eggs should be whipped before being added, for the best results, and the other ingredients put together in the usual order."

Poppyseed Cake

Poppyseed Cake

Basically a pound cake, this recipe contains a generous half-cup of poppy seeds, which add a toasty flavor and a delightful crunch. Seed cake—traditionally made with caraway seed—was a beloved Victorian dessert. Irma Rombauer, author of *Joy of Cooking*, wrote that seed cake reminded her of "antimacassars and aspidistras."

CAKE

3 cups flour

1½ teaspoons baking powder

½ teaspoon salt

3 sticks (12 ounces) butter, softened to
   room temperature

1½ cups granulated sugar

5 eggs

2 teaspoons vanilla extract

½ cup poppy seeds

1 cup sour cream

GLAZE

⅔ cup sifted confectioners' sugar

About 1 tablespoon lemon juice

    1. Make the cake: Preheat the oven to 350°. Butter and flour a Bundt pan or 10-inch tube pan.

    2. In a medium bowl, stir together the flour, baking powder, and salt; set aside.

    3. In a large bowl, cream the butter and granulated sugar until light and fluffy. Beat in the eggs, one at a time, beating well after each addition; then beat in the vanilla.

Beat in the poppy seeds. Alternating between the two, gradually add the dry ingredients and the sour cream, beating well after each addition.

4. Spread the batter evenly in the prepared pan. Rap the pan once or twice on the counter to remove any air pockets. Bake for 50 to 55 minutes, or until the top of the cake springs back when touched, and a toothpick inserted in the center of the cake comes out clean and dry.

5. Let the cake cool in the pan on a rack for 10 minutes, then turn it out onto the rack to cool completely.

6. Meanwhile, make the glaze: In a small bowl, stir together the confectioners' sugar and 1 tablespoon of lemon juice until smooth. Add up to 1 teaspoon more lemon juice, if necessary, to make it pourable. Place the cake on a serving dish, rounded-side up, and drizzle the glaze over the top.   *Makes one 10-inch tube cake*

Apple Cake

When the apple harvest begins, try his homey cake, full of apples, nuts, and raisins. Cinnamon and nutmeg give it a spicy flavor and aroma that are especially welcome in the fall. A square of apple cake is a treat at breakfast or brunch; it's also a comforting dessert, especially topped with a scoop of rum-raisin ice cream.

3 medium Granny Smith or other tart green apples (about 1½ pounds)	*½ teaspoon salt*
¼ cup lemon juice	*1 stick (4 ounces) butter, softened to room temperature*
1 teaspoon grated lemon zest	*⅔ cup (packed) dark brown sugar*
1½ cups flour	*2 eggs, lightly beaten*
1 teaspoon baking soda	*1 cup raisins*
1 teaspoon cinnamon	*1 cup coarsely chopped walnuts*
½ teaspoon grated nutmeg	*1 teaspoon vanillla extract*

1. Preheat the oven to 350°. Butter and flour a 9-inch square baking pan.

2. Peel and finely chop or grate the apples. Place the apples in a bowl, add the lemon juice and zest, and toss well to coat the apples; set aside.

3. In a small bowl, stir together the flour, baking soda, cinnamon, nutmeg, and salt; set aside.

4. In a medium bowl, cream the butter and sugar. Beat in the eggs.

5. Gradually add the dry ingredients, beating well after each addition. Add the apple mixture, the raisins, walnuts, and vanilla, and stir until well blended.

6. Spread the batter evenly in the prepared pan, smoothing the top with a rubber spatula. Rap the pan once or twice on the counter to remove any air pockets. Bake for 45 to 50 minutes, or until the cake shrinks from the sides of the pan and a toothpick inserted in the center of the cake comes out clean and dry.

7. Let the cake cool in the pan on a rack, then cut it into squares and serve it directly from the pan.   *Makes one 9-inch square cake*

The following tip for keeping loaf cakes fresh was contributed by a subscriber to the National Magazine, and was published in Little Helps for Home-Makers in 1909: "I generally cut a loaf of cake in the middle and take as many slices as needed, then bring the two cut surfaces together again, [so] the cake has no cut surface exposed to the air to dry."

Oatmeal Cake

This oatmeal cake, complemented by a warm, crunchy topping, is very popular in the Western states, and may have originated in that part of the country. The topping is a version of "broiled" icing, although this recipe calls for it to be briefly baked instead. If the topping tastes familiar, that's because a similar mixture of butter, brown sugar, coconut, and nuts is used to ice German chocolate cake.

CAKE
1 cup old-fashioned rolled oats
1¼ cups milk, scalded
1 stick (4 ounces) butter, softened to
  room temperature
⅔ cup (packed) dark brown sugar
⅓ cup granulated sugar
2 eggs
1 teaspoon vanilla extract
1 teaspoon baking soda
1 teaspoon cinnamon
½ teaspoon salt

1½ cups flour
1 cup golden raisins
1 cup chopped walnuts

TOPPING
½ cup (packed) brown sugar
2 tablespoons butter, softened to room
  temperature
¼ cup evaporated milk or heavy cream
½ cup sweetened shredded coconut
½ cup chopped walnuts

1. Make the cake: Preheat the oven to 350°. Lightly butter and flour a 13 x 9-inch baking pan.

2. Place the oats in a small bowl and pour the hot milk over them; set aside to cool.

3. In a large bowl, cream the butter and sugars together until very light and fluffy. Beat in the eggs, one at a time, beating well after each addition.

4. Stir in the cooled oatmeal mixture, then add the vanilla, baking soda, cinnamon, and salt. Add the flour, raisins, and nuts, and stir until blended.

5. Spread the batter evenly in the prepared pan, smoothing the top with a rubber spatula. Rap the pan once or twice on the counter to remove any air pockets. Bake for 30 to 35 minutes, or until the cake shrinks from the sides of the pan and a toothpick inserted in the center of the cake comes out clean and dry.

6. A few minutes before the cake is done, make the topping: In a small bowl, cream together the brown sugar and butter. Stir in the evaporated milk, then add the coconut and walnuts, and stir until combined.

7. Spread the topping on the hot cake and return the cake to the oven for 3 minutes, or until the topping is melted. *Makes one 13 x 9-inch cake*

Orange-Chocolate Cake

Here is a cake that will delight those who like their chocolate desserts intensely rich. The velvety frosting is a form of ganache, a confectioner's mixture (often used to make truffles) consisting basically of melted chocolate and cream. Since the recipe calls for nine ounces of chocolate, be sure to use a good-quality product. Experiment with different brands of semisweet and bittersweet chocolate: European brands labeled "extra-bittersweet" are particularly recommended. Marmalades also vary in sweetness; consider trying one of the sharp-flavored English brands, or else one that is prepared with ginger or whiskey.

CAKE
2 cups flour
½ cup unsweetened cocoa powder
1 teaspoon baking powder
¼ teaspoon baking soda
¼ teaspoon salt
1 stick (4 ounces) butter, softened to
    room temperature
1⅓ cups sugar
3 eggs

⅔ cup buttermilk
1 tablespoon grated orange zest
½ teaspoon orange extract

FROSTING AND FILLING
9 ounces semisweet chocolate
1¼ cups sour cream
2 tablespoons confectioners' sugar
½ teaspoon orange extract
½ cup orange marmalade

1. Make the cake: Preheat the oven to 350°. Butter two 8-inch round cake pans and line the bottoms with circles of waxed paper. Butter the waxed paper, then flour the pans.

2. In a small bowl, stir together the flour, cocoa, baking powder, baking soda, and salt.

3. In a large bowl, cream the butter and sugar. Beat in the eggs, one at a time, beating well after each addition. Beat in the buttermilk, orange zest, and orange extract. Add the dry ingredients and beat just until blended; do not overbeat.

4. Spread the batter evenly in the prepared pans. Rap the pans once or twice on the counter to remove any air pockets. Bake for 25 to 30 minutes, or until the cakes shrink from the sides of the pans and a toothpick inserted in the center of each cake comes out clean and dry. Let the cakes cool in the pans for 10 minutes, then turn them out onto racks to cool completely before frosting and filling.

5. Meanwhile, make the frosting: Cut the chocolate into large pieces. In the top of a double boiler over hot, not simmering, water, melt the chocolate, stirring until smooth. Set aside to cool slightly. Stir in the sour cream, confectioners' sugar, and orange extract, and continue stirring until smooth; set aside.

6. For the filling, place the marmalade in a small saucepan and warm it over low heat until it is spreadable.

7. Assemble the cake: Remove the waxed paper from the layers. Spread the marmalade over one cake layer. Top with the second layer, then frost the top and sides of the cake with the chocolate mixture.   *Makes one 8-inch layer cake*

THE PILLSBURY BAKE-OFF

For generations, American cooks have brought their family favorites to country fairs—or prepared them in "cook-offs"—in hopes of a blue ribbon. By far the most famous of these competitions is the Pillsbury Bake-Off, begun in 1949 as the "Grand National Recipe Hunt and Baking Contest," and still flourishing today.

The basic structure of the contest has not changed: from thousands of recipes sent in by home cooks, Pillsbury selects 100 finalists to compete for cash prizes of up to $40,000. In 1949, the only ingredient requirement was that each recipe include a half cup of Pillsbury's flour; since then, categories have been created for other Pillsbury products.

In the contest's first decade, most entrants were full-time housewives, many of whom entered fancifully named "scratch" cakes like Orange Kiss-Me Cake and Blueberry Boy-Bait. But the 1951 Bake-Off saw the first male prizewinner; his entry was Hot Ziggities, a main-dish variation on "pigs in blankets." Few recipes from that era required unusual ingredients, but in 1954, a winner called Open Sesame Pie caused a run on the then-exotic sesame seed, which has been a supermarket staple ever since.

The increasing use of packaged foods in the American household was clearly shown in the Bake-Off recipes of the 1960s. Two entries from that decade were Pantry Stroganoff (made with canned white sauce, French fried onions, and Vienna sausage) and Easy Livin' Caramel Cake (made with potato flakes and frosting mix).

In 1970, the nation's growing health consciousness was reflected in the number of recipes using molasses, whole grains, and wheat germ. Entries included Bran-New Peanut Cookies and Corn Chip Molasses Bread. A main dish, Souper Beef Supper, was awarded a special nutrition prize.

In 1988, each Bake-Off recipe was placed in one of four new divisions: Quick Ideas; Wholesome Alternatives; Ethnic Specialties; or Indulgent Treats. Not surprisingly, these categories summed up the contemporary American appetite—including an undying passion for sweets. Trendy recipes from the late 1980s included Easy Vegetable Bulgur Salad and Chocolate Praline Layer Cake.

Raspberry Cheesecake

Although it has become an American restaurant mainstay, cheesecake originated in Europe. Martha Washington's recipe, recorded in the handwritten family cookbook she inherited, called for "new milk" and rennet (added to turn the milk into cheese), butter, cream, sugar, currants, rosewater, and nutmeg.

1 package (8½ ounces) chocolate wafers
⅓ cup butter, melted
2 packages (8 ounces each) cream cheese,
  softened to room temperature
¾ cup sugar
1 tablespoon flour

1 cup sour cream
3 eggs
3 tablespoons lemon juice, preferably fresh
2 teaspoons vanilla extract
¼ cup seedless raspberry jam
½ pint fresh raspberries

1. Preheat the oven to 350°.

2. Make the crust: In a food processor or blender, process the chocolate wafers to fine crumbs; transfer the crumbs to a bowl. Add the melted butter and stir to combine, then pat the crumb mixture into the bottom and halfway up the sides of an 8½-inch springform pan; set aside.

3. Make the filling: In a medium bowl, beat the cream cheese and sugar until smooth. Beat in the flour, then the sour cream. Beat in the eggs, one at a time, beating well after each addition.

4. Add the lemon juice and vanilla, and beat until smooth. Pour the filling into the crust (the filling will rise above the crust). Bake for 1 hour to 1 hour and 10 minutes, or until the filling is set. Let the cake cool completely in the pan on a rack.

5. To serve, place the pan on a serving platter and remove the rim of the pan. Warm the jam in a small saucepan over low heat just until it is pourable. Arrange the raspberries decoratively on top of the cake and spoon the jam over them.

Makes one 8½-inch cake

Mississippi Mud Cake

As dark and rich as its namesake, this cake is especially tempting when accompanied by dollops of softly whipped, lightly sweetened cream.

¼ cup unsweetened cocoa powder plus
   extra for dusting the pan
4 ounces unsweetened chocolate
2 sticks (8 ounces) butter
1½ cups strong brewed coffee
¼ cup bourbon

1¾ cups flour
½ teaspoon baking soda
⅛ teaspoon salt
1½ cups sugar
2 eggs
1 teaspoon vanilla extract

1. Preheat the oven to 325°. Butter a Bundt pan or 10-inch tube pan and dust it with some cocoa powder.

2. Cut the chocolate into large pieces. In the top of a double boiler combine the chocolate, butter, coffee, and bourbon. Heat over hot, not simmering, water, stirring occasionally, until the butter and chocolate melt.

3. Meanwhile, in a medium bowl, stir together the flour, remaining ¼ cup cocoa, the baking soda, and salt. Set aside.

4. When the chocolate mixture is melted and smooth, transfer it to a large bowl. Begin to beat it at low speed, adding the sugar a little at a time, and continue beating until the sugar is thoroughly incorporated.

5. Gradually beat in the dry ingredients, beating well after each addition. Beat in the eggs, one at a time, and the vanilla, and beat until smooth.

6. Spread the batter evenly in the prepared pan. Rap the pan once or twice on the counter to remove any air pockets. Bake for 40 to 45 minutes, or until the cake shrinks from the sides of the pan and a toothpick inserted in the center of the cake comes out clean and dry.

7. Let the cake cool completely in the pan on a rack before turning it out onto a serving plate.

Makes one 10-inch tube cake

Dark Gingerbread

Nineteenth-century farm families ate hearty breakfasts and midday dinners, but supper—eaten just before bedtime—was usually a light meal. Frequently, pie, mush, or gingerbread with butter or applesauce was served as the main dish in the evening.

2 cups flour
1 tablespoon unsweetened cocoa powder
1½ teaspoons baking soda
2½ teaspoons ground ginger
½ teapoon allspice
¼ teaspoon salt

⅔ cup molasses
⅔ cup sour cream
1 stick (4 ounces) butter, softened to room
   temperature
½ cup (packed) dark brown sugar
2 eggs, lightly beaten

1. Preheat the oven to 350°. Butter and flour a 9 x 9-inch baking pan.

2. In a small bowl, stir together the flour, cocoa, baking soda, ginger, allspice, and salt. In another small bowl, stir together the molasses and sour cream.

3. In a large bowl, cream the butter and sugar until smooth. Add the eggs and beat until blended. Alternating between the two, add the dry ingredients and the molasses mixture, beating well after each addition.

4. Spread the batter evenly in the prepared pan. Rap the pan once or twice on the counter to remove any air pockets. Bake for 30 to 35 minutes, or until the cake shrinks from the sides of the pan and a toothpick inserted in the center of the gingerbread comes out clean and dry.

5. Let the gingerbread cool in the pan on a rack, then cut it into squares and serve warm, or at room temperature.

Makes one 9-inch square cake

1-2-3-4 Cake

Before standardized measures were commonly used, recipes often called for ingredients by the teacup, coffee cup, tumbler, or wineglass. In an attempt to make their recipes more fail-safe, some cookbooks specified proportions—rather than precise quantities—of ingredients. The name of this early-American cake helped the cook remember the proportions—one part butter, two parts sugar, three parts flour, and four eggs—whatever size measure might be used.

3 cups flour

2 teaspoons baking powder

½ teaspoon salt

4 eggs, separated

2 sticks (8 ounces) butter, softened to
  room temperature

2 cups sugar

1 cup milk

1 teaspoon grated lemon zest

1 teaspoon vanilla extract

1. Preheat the oven to 350°. Butter and flour a 13 x 9-inch baking pan.

2. Sift the flour, baking powder, and salt into a medium bowl, and stir to mix.

3. In a medium bowl, beat the egg whites until stiff peaks form.

4. In a large bowl, cream the butter and sugar. Beat in the egg yolks until well blended. Alternating between the two, add the dry ingredients and the milk, beating well after each addition. Add the lemon zest and vanilla, and stir until well blended. Fold one-fourth of the beaten egg whites into the batter, then fold in the remaining egg whites.

5. Spread the batter evenly in the prepared pan. Rap the pan once or twice on the counter to remove any air pockets. Bake for 40 to 45 minutes, or until the cake shrinks from the sides of the pan and a toothpick inserted in the center of the cake comes out clean and dry.

6. Let the cake cool in the pan on a rack, then cut it into squares.

Makes one 13 x 9-inch cake

Chocolate-Chip Devil's-Food Cake

For many families, chocolate layer cake, rather than apple pie, represents the quintessential American dessert. Chocolate-loving American cooks have devised countless luscious variations of devil's-food cake. The chocolate chips in this version make it doubly rich, while dark brown sugar, an unusual ingredient in a chocolate cake, intensifies its overall flavor and moistness.

CAKE
4 ounces unsweetened chocolate
1 cup milk
2¼ cups flour
1 teaspoon baking powder
¼ teaspoon salt
1 stick (4 ounces) butter, softened to
    room temperature
1⅓ cups (packed) dark brown sugar
3 eggs

1 teaspoon vanilla extract
1½ cups chocolate chips

FROSTING
¾ cup granulated sugar
½ cup (packed) light brown sugar
1 cup heavy cream
4 ounces unsweetened chocolate
1 stick (4 ounces) butter, cut into pieces

1. Make the cake: Preheat the oven to 350°. Butter two 8-inch round cake pans and line the bottoms with circles of waxed paper. Butter the waxed paper, then flour the pans.

2. Cut the unsweetened chocolate into large pieces. In the top of a double boiler, over hot, not simmering, water, melt the chocolate in ¼ cup of the milk, stirring until smooth. Set aside to cool slightly.

3. In a small bowl, stir together the flour, baking powder, and salt; set aside.

4. In a large bowl, cream the butter and dark brown sugar. Beat in the eggs, one at a time, beating well after each addition, then beat in the vanilla. Beat in the cooled chocolate mixture and the remaining ¾ cup milk. Beat in the dry ingredients, then stir in the chocolate chips.

5. Spread the batter evenly in the prepared pans. Rap the pans once or twice on the counter to remove any air pockets. Bake for 30 to 35 minutes, or until the cake shrinks from the sides of the pans and a toothpick inserted in the center of each cake comes out clean and dry. Let the cakes cool in the pans for 10 minutes, then turn them out onto racks to cool completely.

6. Meanwhile, make the frosting: In a small, heavy saucepan, bring the granulated and brown sugars and the cream to a boil over medium heat, stirring constantly. Reduce the heat so that the mixture just simmers, and cook, without stirring, for 6 minutes. Meanwhile, cut the chocolate into large pieces.

7. Remove the pan from the heat, add the chocolate and butter, and stir until melted. Beat the frosting until cooled, thick, and creamy, 12 to 15 minutes.

8. Frost the cake: Remove the waxed paper from the layers. Spread a generous layer of frosting over one cake layer. Top with the second layer, then frost the top and sides of the cake.

Makes one 8-inch layer cake

A 19th-century Sunday-night supper, as remembered by Della Lutes (a Michigan farmer's daughter) in her book Home Grown, was a very special occasion: "When flowers were scarce, a handsome cake often had the place of honor—a cake made specially for the purpose by one of the girls on Saturday; perhaps a round layer cake, oozing rich dark chocolate, with a smooth glazed coat of the same; a moist and velvety bed of cake resting on a high-posted dish of glass with a slightly rolled edge to keep the cake in place."

Chocolate-Chip Devil's-Food Cake

SPICE BOXES

Spices were something of a luxury in colonial America. Indeed, the spice repertoire of that era consisted of little more than cinnamon, nutmeg, cloves, mace, ginger, pepper, and allspice. These precious seasonings were carefully stored to preserve their volatile flavors.

Until the mid-19th century, spices were only sold whole, dispensed from caddies into paper wrappings. At home, they were transferred to a container, such as a wooden spice chest fitted with drawers. Some of these diminutive boxes were created as cabinetmaker's samples, fashioned to display the craftsman's mastery of furniture styles; others were more humble homemade affairs.

Some cooks preferred to store their spices in individual tins or boxes. These might be sold in sets, fitted into a larger box for storage (or carrying). Sets of round wooden boxes, made of bentwood, resemble Shaker pantry boxes; other spice sets were made of tin. One early, unusual spice-keeper consisted of a stacking set of round wooden canisters: each one screwed onto the one below. (Two of these are seen in the photograph at right.) More decorative sets of tins or jars, arranged in racks, became popular in the 19th century and remain kitchen standards today.

Around 1850, preground spices began to be sold in small round tins with paper labels; later, the shaker top was added. Rectangular tins with labels printed directly onto the metal surface—similar to the spice containers sold in supermarkets today—soon supplanted the round ones.

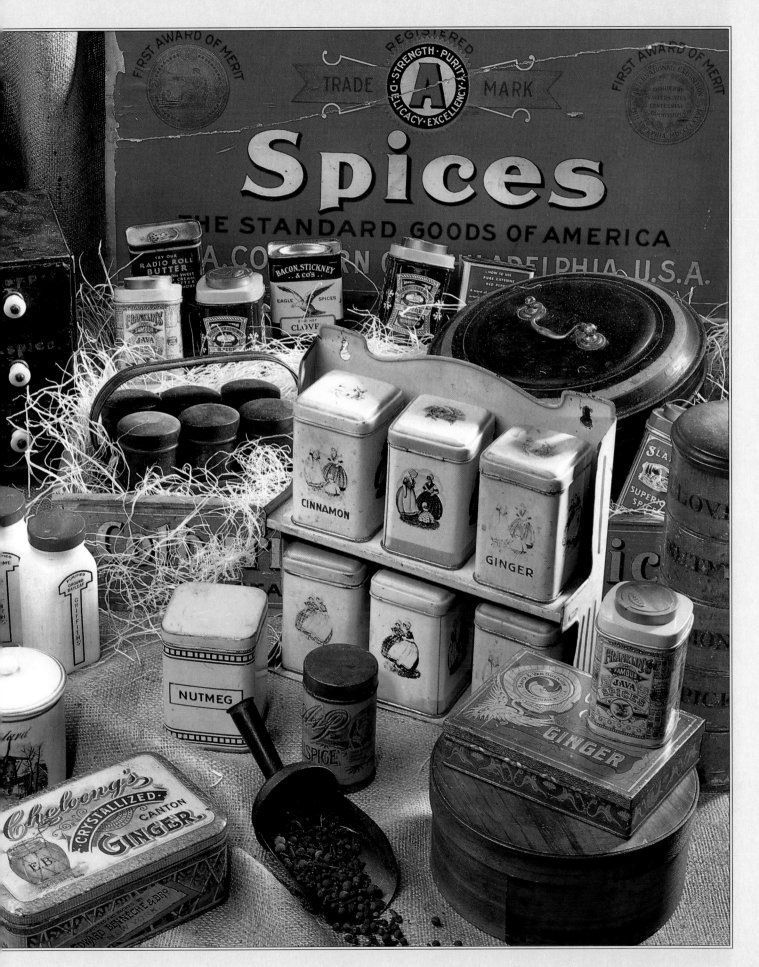

Fresh Peach Cake

The complementary flavors of peaches and almonds (both members of the botanical family *prunus*) suffuse this lofty layer cake: The filling is an almond-scented custard topped with a layer of sliced peaches. Make this cake on the day it is to be served, as the delicate filling and whipped cream frosting will not keep well.

The birthday of Mother Ann Lee, founder of the Shakers, was celebrated every year with a peach cake, known as Mother Ann's Birthday Cake. It was a white cake, baked in layers and put together with peach jam. For extra flavor, the batter was beaten with bruised peach twigs, which were said to "impart a delicate peach flavor to the cake."

CAKE
1¾ cups sifted cake flour
1 teaspoon baking powder
¼ teaspoon salt
7 eggs, separated
1⅔ cups granulated sugar
1 teaspoon almond extract
¼ cup milk
½ teaspoon cream of tartar

CUSTARD AND PEACH FILLING
1 cup milk

4 egg yolks
½ cup granulated sugar
3 tablespoons all-purpose flour
¼ teaspoon almond extract
1 medium peach
1 tablespoon lemon juice

FROSTING AND GARNISH
1 cup sliced almonds, toasted
1 cup heavy cream
¼ cup sifted confectioners' sugar
1 medium peach, unpeeled

1. Make the cake: Preheat the oven to 350°. Butter the bottoms of two 9-inch round cake pans and line them with circles of waxed paper. Butter and flour the waxed paper.

2. In a small bowl, stir together the cake flour, baking powder, and salt.

3. In a large bowl, beat the egg yolks and granulated sugar until pale and lemon-colored. Beat in the almond extract. Alternating between the two, gradually beat in the flour mixture and the milk, beating well after each addition.

4. In a medium bowl, beat the egg whites until frothy. Add the cream of tartar and continue beating until stiff peaks form. Gently fold one-fourth of the beaten egg whites into the batter, then fold in the remaining egg whites.

5. Spread the batter evenly in the prepared pans. Rap the pans once or twice on the counter to remove any air pockets. Bake for about 30 minutes, or until the cakes shrink from the sides of the pans and a toothpick inserted in the center of each cake comes out clean and dry. Let the cakes cool in the pans for 10 minutes, then turn them out onto racks to cool completely before filling and frosting them.

6. Meanwhile, make the custard: In a small saucepan, scald the milk. In the top of a double boiler, combine the egg yolks, granulated sugar, and all-purpose flour, and stir until smooth. Slowly drizzle in the hot milk. Place the double boiler over simmering water and cook, stirring, until the custard thickens, about 5 minutes.

7. Remove the double boiler from the heat and stir in the almond extract. Let cool slightly, then cover the custard with plastic wrap, placing the plastic directly on the surface of the custard to prevent a skin from forming. Set the custard aside to cool to room temperature, then refrigerate it until ready to use.

8. Meanwhile, peel and slice the peach: Bring a small saucepan of water to a boil. Blanch the peach in the boiling water for about 1 minute. Drain the peach and cool it

Fresh Peach Cake

briefly under cold running water, then peel and cut it into ¼-inch-thick slices. Place the peach slices in a bowl, add the lemon juice, and toss to coat the slices thoroughly; set aside.

9. Make the frosting: Preheat the oven to 375°. Place the almonds on an ungreased baking sheet and toast, stirring occasionally, until golden, 5 to 10 minutes. Set aside to cool slightly.

10. Meanwhile, in a large bowl, beat the cream until soft peaks form, then beat in the confectioners' sugar just until stiff peaks form. Reserving the lemon juice, drain the sliced peaches.

11. Assemble the cake: Remove the waxed paper from the layers. Spread half of the cooled custard evenly over one cake layer. Arrange the peeled peach slices on top of the custard, then spoon the remaining custard over the slices. Place the second cake layer on top and frost the entire cake with whipped cream. Decorate the frosting with the toasted almonds. Slice the remaining unpeeled peach and toss the slices with the reserved lemon juice. Drain the peach slices and pat them dry. Arrange them decoratively on top of the cake.   *Makes one 9-inch layer cake*

Kentucky Bourbon Cake

Many old recipes for pound cake include brandy, but the cook who first substituted bourbon whiskey created a Kentucky classic. Mace, which is derived from the outer covering of the nutmeg kernel, is another traditional flavoring for pound cake. If it is not readily available, ground nutmeg makes an acceptable substitute.

2 cups raisins
1/2 cup bourbon
2 cups flour
1 teaspoon ground mace or nutmeg
3/4 teaspoon baking soda
1/4 teaspoon salt
1 1/2 sticks (6 ounces) butter, softened to room temperature

1/2 cup (packed) dark brown sugar
1/2 cup granulated sugar
4 eggs
1/2 cup molasses
1 teaspoon vanilla extract
2 cups chopped pecans, plus 3/4 cup pecan halves

1. Preheat the oven to 350°. Butter a 10-inch tube pan and line the bottom with a ring of waxed paper. Butter the waxed paper.
2. Place the raisins in a small bowl and pour 1/4 cup of the bourbon over them. Set aside to soak for at least 1 hour, stirring occasionally. Reserving the bourbon, drain the raisins; set aside.
3. In a small bowl, stir together the flour, mace, baking soda, and salt.
4. In a large bowl, cream the butter and the brown and granulated sugars. Add the eggs, one at a time, beating well after each addition. Add the molasses, vanilla, and the bourbon used to soak the raisins.
5. Gradually add the dry ingredients, beating well after each addition. Fold in the chopped pecans and the drained raisins.
6. Spread the batter evenly in the prepared pan. Rap the pan once or twice on the counter to remove any air pockets. Arrange the pecans halves decoratively on top of the batter and bake for 50 to 55 minutes, or until the cake shrinks from the sides of the pan and a toothpick inserted in the center of the cake comes out clean and dry.
7. Let the cake cool in the pan for 30 minutes. Turn the cake out onto a plate and remove the waxed paper. Then invert the cake onto a rack, right-side up, to cool completely.
8. Place the cake in an airtight container and drape a sheet of cheesecloth over the cake. Slowly pour the remaining 1/4 cup bourbon over the cloth and cake, close the container tightly, and store for up to 3 months. *Makes one 10-inch tube cake*

Banana-Coconut Cake

Here is a luxurious version of the popular Southern coconut cake. A moist coconut sponge cake is layered with a whipped cream-banana filling and frosted with drifts of whipped cream and more coconut. Since the whipped cream doesn't keep well, the cake should be served the day it is made.

CAKE	FILLING AND FROSTING
1⅓ cups cake flour	2 small bananas
¾ teaspoon baking powder	1 tablespoon lime juice
¼ teaspoon salt	1½ cups heavy cream
5 eggs, separated	¼ cup sifted confectioners' sugar
1¼ cups granulated sugar	1½ cups sweetened shredded coconut
3 tablespoons milk	
½ teaspoon coconut extract	
1 cup sweetened shredded coconut	
½ teaspoon cream of tartar	

1. Make the cake: Preheat the oven to 350°. Butter the bottoms of two 8-inch round cake pans and line them with circles of waxed paper. Butter and flour the waxed paper.

2. In a small bowl, stir together the flour, baking powder, and salt.

3. In a large bowl, beat the egg yolks and granulated sugar until pale and lemon-colored. Beat in the milk and the coconut extract. Gradually beat in the dry ingredients, beating well after each addition. Stir in the coconut.

4. In a medium bowl, beat the egg whites until frothy. Add the cream of tartar and continue beating until stiff peaks form. Gently fold one-fourth of the beaten egg whites into the batter, then fold in the remaining egg whites.

5. Spread the batter evenly in the prepared pans. Rap the pans once or twice on the counter to remove any air pockets. Bake for 25 to 30 minutes, or until the cakes shrink from the sides of the pans and a toothpick inserted in the center of each cake comes out clean and dry. Let the cakes cool in the pans for 10 minutes, then turn them out onto racks to cool completely before filling and frosting them.

6. Meanwhile, make the filling and frosting: Peel and slice the bananas and place them in a small bowl. Add the lime juice and toss to coat the bananas thoroughly. In a large bowl, beat the cream until soft peaks form, then beat in the confectioners' sugar. Add 1 cup of the whipped cream to the banana mixture and fold gently to combine.

7. Assemble the cake: Remove the waxed paper from the layers. Spread the banana-whipped cream mixture evenly over the one cake layer. Top with the second layer, then frost the top and sides of the cake with the remaining whipped cream. Sprinkle the coconut over the whipped cream. Refrigerate the cake until ready to serve.

Makes one 8-inch layer cake

Cookies

*perennial family favorites
and special-occasion treats*

Was there ever a cookie jar with a quiet cover? One of the rewards of making cookies is the sound of lid against jar as eager hands return for yet another treat. Homemade cookies are the stuff of memories: the aromas of cinnamon, nutmeg, and vanilla; the familiar motions of chopping nuts, creaming butter, and shaping dough; and the first bite of a first-batch sample still hot from the oven.

It is not surprising that baking—and eating—cookies has become a national passion. Whether your favorite is oatmeal cookies, gingersnaps, sugar cookies, or snickerdoodles, no country kitchen seems quite complete without some of these popular treats on hand. This chapter explores a rich range of cookie possibilities, from lunchbox standbys such as hermits and brownies to more elegant delicacies like pecan lace wafers and lemon jam squares. Ideas for holiday baking are here, too: gingerbread, spritz, and two-tone icebox cookies are sure to brighten any festive gathering.

Homemade preserves are put to good use in Jam Thumbprints.

Fruit Fold-Ups

The filling for these cookies can be made from just about any combination of dried fruits. Health-food stores and gourmet shops usually stock dried apples, apricots, peaches, pineapple, dates, figs, currants, and cherries. If you choose one of the sweeter fruits, such as pineapple, use a little less sugar when making the filling.

COOKIE DOUGH
1½ cups all-purpose flour
½ cup whole wheat flour
2 tablespoons dark brown sugar
1 teaspoon baking powder
½ teaspoon baking soda
¼ teaspoon salt
1½ sticks (6 ounces) chilled butter, cut
 into pieces

1 egg, lightly beaten
1 teaspoon vanilla extract

FILLING
4 cups mixed dried fruits
1½ cups (packed) dark brown sugar
⅔ cup apple juice
3 tablespoons honey

1. Make the cookie dough: In a large bowl, stir together the all-purpose and whole-wheat flours, the brown sugar, baking powder, baking soda, and salt. Using a pastry blender or two knives, cut in the butter until the mixture resembles cornmeal. Add the egg and vanilla, and stir until the mixture forms a firm dough.

2. Shape the dough into a ball, turn it out onto a sheet of plastic wrap, and flatten it slightly. Wrap the dough and refrigerate it until ready to use.

3. Make the filling: In a medium saucepan, combine the dried fruits, sugar, apple

Fruit Fold-Ups

juice, and honey. Cook over medium heat, stirring occasionally, until the mixture comes to a boil. Cover the pan, reduce the heat, and simmer the mixture for 10 to 15 minutes, or until the fruits are softened. Set aside to cool completely.

4. In a food processor or blender, process the fruit mixture until uniformly chopped but not completely smooth. Transfer the filling to a bowl, cover it with plastic wrap, and refrigerate it for at least 30 minutes, or until well chilled.

5. Preheat the oven to 375°.

6. Cut the dough into two equal portions. On a lightly floured surface, using a lightly floured rolling pin, roll out each portion of dough to a 15 x 6½-inch rectangle. Spoon a 3-inch-wide strip of filling down the center of each rectangle of dough, leaving a ½-inch border at each end.

7. Using a long metal spatula, fold both sides of the dough lengthwise over the filling, and press the edges lightly to seal them. Turn the filled loaves seam-side down, then press them gently to flatten them to a width of about 3 inches. Using the spatula, transfer the loaves to an ungreased baking sheet, leaving at least 1 inch of space between them, and bake for 20 to 25 minutes, or until golden brown.

8. Let cool on the baking sheet for 15 minutes, then transfer the loaves to a rack to cool completely. When cool, transfer to a cutting board and cut each loaf into ¾-inch-wide slices.

Makes about 40 cookies

Jam Thumbprints

Let the children "lend a hand" with these rich and buttery cookies. Even the youngest can make the thumbprints and pick their favorite jams and jellies for filling them.

1 stick (4 ounces) butter, softened to room temperature	1 teaspoon vanilla extract
⅓ cup sugar	1⅓ cups flour
1 egg yolk	¼ cup jam, jelly, or marmalade
	⅓ cup slivered blanched almonds

1. Preheat the oven to 350°. Lightly grease a baking sheet.

2. In a large bowl, cream the butter until smooth and light. Add the sugar and beat until light and fluffy, then beat in the egg yolk and vanilla. Gradually add the flour and mix until completely incorporated. The dough should be very firm.

3. Shape the dough into 1-inch balls and place them on the prepared baking sheet, leaving 2 inches of space between them. With your thumb, make a deep indentation in the center of each cookie. Bake for 7 to 9 minutes, or until firm.

4. Remove the baking sheet from the oven and fill the center of each cookie with about ½ teaspoon of jam, then sprinkle the jam with the slivered almonds. Return the cookies to the oven and bake for 6 to 8 minutes longer, or until they are light golden brown around the edges.

5. Let the cookies cool on the baking sheet for 2 to 3 minutes, then transfer them to a rack to cool.

Makes about 2 dozen

A turn-of-the century tip for keeping soft cookies moist still works perfectly well today: Put a layer of cookies into a cookie jar, "then a slice of bread, then more cookies, then bread, until you have them all in. The bread will become dry and the cakes keep moist. Replenish the bread if it gets very dry." Slices of fresh apple, loosely wrapped in waxed paper, will also do the trick.

Gingerbread Cookies

Gingerbread Cookies

Although gingerbread figures are a symbol of Christmas, it's fun to bake these cookies in other shapes for other holidays and special occasions. Indeed today, cookie cutters can be found in many designs, from dinosaurs to dump trucks. If you have antique cookie cutters, don't be afraid to use them for baking. Just be sure to dry them well after washing so that they do not rust. See Royal Icing Decoration (pages 88-89) for some cookie-decorating ideas.

COOKIES

1 stick (4 ounces) butter
1/3 cup molasses
1/2 cup (packed) light brown sugar
1 tablespoon ground ginger
1/2 teaspoon cinnamon
1/2 teaspoon ground cloves
1/2 teaspoon nutmeg
1/2 teaspoon baking soda
1 egg, lightly beaten

2 1/2 cups flour
1/4 teaspoon baking powder
1/4 teaspoon salt

DECORATION AND ICING

Dried fruits, cut into small pieces
1 1/4 cups confectioners' sugar
2 tablespoons water
1/4 teaspoon vanilla extract

1. Preheat the oven to 325°. Lightly grease a baking sheet.

2. Cut the butter into 1-inch pieces and place them in a large bowl.

3. In a medium saucepan, bring the molasses, brown sugar, ginger, cinnamon, cloves, and nutmeg to a low boil, stirring occasionally. Add the baking soda and stir until the mixture foams up in the saucepan, 1 to 2 minutes.

4. Pour the hot molasses mixture over the butter and stir to melt the butter. Add the egg and stir to blend. Gradually stir in the flour, baking powder, and salt.

5. Turn the dough out onto a lightly floured surface and knead it lightly until the dough is smooth; form it into a ball. Using a lightly floured rolling pin, roll the dough out to a 1/4-inch thickness.

6. Cut out the cookies using floured cookie cutters. Place the cookies on the prepared baking sheet, leaving 1 inch of space between them. Gather, reroll, and cut the scraps of dough.

7. Decorate the cookies with bits of the dried fruits. If you plan to string the cookies on ribbons for hanging, use a skewer or ice pick to make small holes at the tops. Bake the cookies for 13 to 15 minutes, or until crisp.

8. Let the cookies cool on the baking sheet for 2 to 3 minutes, then transfer them to a rack to cool completely.

9. Meanwhile, prepare the icing: In a small bowl, combine the confectioners' sugar, water, and vanilla, and stir until thick and smooth; set aside.

10. Fill a pastry bag with the icing and pipe it onto the cookies. Add details with more bits of the dried fruits, if desired.

Makes about 2 dozen

COOKIE MOLDS

Simple or elaborate works of edible art, cookies made with molds are a centuries-old Northern European specialty brought to this country in the 17th and 18th centuries and long since adopted—and adapted—by American cooks.

The most common type of molded cookie is one made with a dough stiff enough to retain the mold's image. From the British Isles come recipes for spicy gingerbread and rich Scottish shortbread; from Germany come such holiday treats as *springerle* (hard anise-flavored cookies) and *lebkuchen* (honey cakes); and from other parts of Northern Europe come gingerbread-like cookies such as Swiss *tirggel* and *leckerli*, and Dutch *speculaas*.

Cookie molds—both antique and modern—come in a variety of forms. Individual wood, glass, or ceramic stamps are used to press designs into one cookie at a time. Carved wooden or cast-metal rolling pins, and wooden "cake prints," can mass-produce sheets of embossed dough. There are also shaped molds, usually ceramic, in which the dough is actually baked, giving the cookies a distinctive silhouette as well as a raised design.

Among the cookie molds at right are an antique cast-metal rolling pin (middle, right), a modern cast-iron cookie pan (top, right), and two wooden shortbread molds: a modern one with a thistle design (top, center) and an antique mold (bottom, center) with the words "The World's Delicious Shortbread" carved in the bottom.

Chocolate-Drizzled Toffee Bars

Chocolate-Drizzled Toffee Bars

A buttery crust, toasted-almond topping, and chocolate glaze give these cookies a sophisticated richness. Serve them for tea, or as an elegant dessert with demitasse.

CRUST
2 sticks (8 ounces) butter, softened to
  room temperature
1 cup granulated sugar
1 egg
2 cups flour

NUT TOPPING
1 cup whole unblanched almonds

4 tablespoons butter, softened to room
  temperature
⅔ cup (packed) dark brown sugar
1 teaspoon vanilla extract

CHOCOLATE GLAZE
2 ounces semisweet chocolate
1 tablespoon vegetable shortening
½ teaspoon vanilla extract

1. Preheat the oven to 300°. Grease and flour an 11 x 7-inch baking pan.
2. Make the crust: In a medium bowl, cream the butter and granulated sugar. Beat in the egg, then add the flour and mix until blended. Spread the dough evenly in the bottom of the prepared pan and bake for 20 minutes. Set the crust aside to cool slightly and increase the oven temperature to 350°.

3. Meanwhile, make the nut topping: Place the almonds in an ungreased, heavy skillet and toast them over medium-high heat, shaking the pan frequently, until golden brown, 5 to 10 minutes. Briefly cool, then coarsely chop the almonds.

4. In a small saucepan, combine the butter and brown sugar. Cook over medium heat, stirring frequently, until the butter melts and the sugar dissolves. Remove the pan from the heat and stir in the vanilla.

5. Spread the sugar mixture evenly over the crust. Sprinkle the chopped almonds on top and bake for another 20 minutes, or until the topping is set.

6. Meanwhile, make the chocolate glaze: In the top of a double boiler over hot, not simmering, water, melt the chocolate and vegetable shortening and stir until smooth. Stir in the vanilla.

7. Drizzle the chocolate glaze over the nut topping. Let cool in the pan on a rack, then cut into 20 bars. *Makes 20*

Toasted Almond Brownies

Though cakelike in texture, these brownies are undeniably rich—a half pound of chocolate guarantees an intense flavor. For a crunchy texture, crisp pan-toasted almonds are added instead of the more commonly used walnuts or pecans.

½ cup chopped almonds	*2 sticks (8 ounces) butter, softened to*
4 ounces semisweet chocolate	*room temperature*
4 ounces unsweetened chocolate	*1⅔ cups sugar*
1 cup flour	*3 eggs*
1 teaspoon baking powder	*1 teaspoon vanilla extract*
¼ teaspoon salt	

1. Preheat the oven to 350°. Grease and flour an 11 x 7-inch baking pan.

2. Toast the almonds in a small, heavy skillet over medium-high heat, shaking the pan frequently, until golden brown, 5 to 10 minutes; set aside to cool slightly.

3. Meanwhile, cut the semisweet and unsweetened chocolate into large pieces. In the top of a double boiler over hot, not simmering, water, melt the chocolate, stirring until smooth. Set aside to cool slightly.

4. In a small bowl, stir together the flour, baking powder, and salt.

5. In a large bowl, cream the butter and sugar until light and fluffy. Beat in the eggs, one at a time, beating well after each addition. Beat in the vanilla. Add the melted chocolate and mix until well blended, then gradually add the dry ingredients, beating well after each addition. Stir in the almonds.

6. Spread the batter evenly in the prepared pan. Rap the pan once or twice on the counter to remove any air pockets. Bake for 45 to 50 minutes, or until the brownies shrink from the sides of the pan, and a toothpick inserted in the center comes out clean and dry.

7. Let cool in the pan on a rack, then cut into 20 bars. *Makes 20*

The term "brownie" has not always been applied to a fudgy bar cookie. Some 19th-century brownies (including Fannie Farmer's) were made with chopped nuts, but no chocolate; others were drop cookies; and some bar cookies resembling modern-day brownies were called "Indians." But by 1906, a published recipe similar to the brownies we know and love today concluded: "These 'Brownies' are a pleasing addition . . . when serving refreshments and will keep some time, if you hide them."

Hermits

These mysterious-sounding New England cookies—named, perhaps, in tribute to their good keeping qualities—are a favorite in lunchboxes and picnic baskets.

2 cups flour
1 teaspoon cinnamon
½ teaspoon allspice
½ teaspoon nutmeg
½ teaspoon baking powder
¼ teaspoon salt
1 stick (4 ounces) butter, softened to
*   room temperature*

¾ cup (packed) dark brown sugar
2 eggs
¼ cup molasses
1 teaspoon vanilla extract
1 cup golden raisins
1 cup coarsely chopped walnuts

1. Preheat the oven to 350°. Lightly grease a baking sheet.
2. In a small bowl, stir together the flour, cinnamon, allspice, nutmeg, baking powder, and salt.
3. In a large bowl, cream the butter and sugar until light and fluffy. Beat in the eggs, one at a time, beating well after each addition. Beat in the molasses and the vanilla. Gradually add the dry ingredients, beating well after each addition until the dough is smooth. Stir in the raisins and walnuts.
4. Drop the cookie dough by the tablespoon onto the prepared baking sheet, leaving 2 inches of space between them. Bake for 15 to 17 minutes, or until the cookies are lightly browned on the edges.
5. Cool the cookies on a rack.

Makes about 4 dozen

Apricot-Nut Bars

Part of the mixture used for the bottom crust is sprinkled on top of these bars, like a crunchy walnut streusel. The filling is made of dried apricots cooked with apple juice and brown sugar.

1½ cups dried apricots
½ cup apple juice
¼ cup (packed) light brown sugar
1½ cups flour
½ teaspoon baking soda

¼ teaspoon salt
1 stick (4 ounces) chilled butter, cut into pieces
1 cup chopped walnuts
⅓ cup granulated sugar
2 teaspoons grated orange zest

1. Preheat the oven to 350°. Grease and flour an 8-inch square baking pan.
2. In a small saucepan, combine the apricots, apple juice, and brown sugar, and bring to a boil over medium heat. Cover the pan, reduce the heat to medium-low, and simmer the mixture until the apricots are tender, about 10 minutes. Remove the pan from the heat and set aside, uncovered, to cool slightly.

3. Transfer the apricot mixture to a food processor or blender and process, pulsing the machine on and off, until the mixture is a spreadable consistency, 5 to 10 seconds. Set the filling aside.

4. Make the crust: In a medium bowl, stir together the flour, baking soda, and salt. Using a pastry blender or two knives, cut in the butter until the mixture resembles cornmeal. Stir in the walnuts, sugar, and orange zest; the mixture will be crumbly.

5. Set aside ⅔ cup of the crust mixture for the topping, then pat the remaining mixture evenly over the bottom of the prepared baking pan. Bake the crust for 10 minutes, or until firm.

6. Carefully spread the apricot filling over the crust, then sprinkle the reserved crust mixture evenly over the filling. Bake for another 25 to 30 minutes, or until the topping is golden.

7. Let cool in the pan on a rack, then cut into 20 bars. *Makes 20*

Snickerdoodles

Although the word sounds as if it might have German origins, "snickerdoodle" is probably just another pleasingly nonsensical cookie name, like "Joe Froggers" and "Lizzies." Comfortingly homey, with warm spices, walnuts, and raisins, these tasty treats might also be called "sugar, spice, and everything nice" cookies.

2½ cups flour
1 teaspoon baking soda
1 teaspoon cream of tartar
2 teaspoons cinnamon
½ teaspoon nutmeg
¼ teaspoon salt
2 sticks (8 ounces) butter, softened to
  room temperature

1½ cups sugar
2 eggs
1 teaspoon vanilla extract
1 cup raisins
1 cup coarsely chopped walnuts

1. Preheat the oven to 375°. Lightly grease a baking sheet.

2. In a small bowl, stir together the flour, baking soda, cream of tartar, 1 teaspoon of the cinnamon, the nutmeg, and salt.

3. In a large bowl, cream the butter and 1¼ cups of the sugar until light and fluffy. Beat in the eggs, one at a time, beating well after each addition. Beat in the vanilla. Gradually add the dry ingredients, beating well after each addition. Stir in the raisins and walnuts.

4. In a shallow bowl, stir together the remaining ¼ cup sugar and 1 teaspoon cinnamon. Shape the dough into 1-inch balls, then roll them in the cinnamon sugar. Place the balls on the prepared baking sheet, leaving 2 inches of space between them. Bake for 12 to 15 minutes, or until the cookies have spread and are lightly browned around the edges.

5. Cool the cookies on a rack. *Makes 5 to 6 dozen*

Fold a square (at least 15 inches) of parchment or freezer paper in half diagonally. Unfold the paper and cut it along the fold to form two triangles.

With the base of a triangle toward you, bring the right-hand point up to meet the apex, twisting the paper so that a cone begins to form.

Bring the other side of the triangle around to the back of the cone. Tape or staple the points in place. Holding the cone, spoon the icing in.

Royal Icing Decoration

Royal icing can transform simple cookies into special treats to be given as holiday gifts or used as ornaments or placecards. Working with a paper cone (see step-by-step photos at left), you can draw intricate patterns with this smooth, easily controllable icing.

The designs shown here (taken from a 19th-century quilt) were applied in the manner of cloisonné enameling: an outline was drawn with royal icing, using the paper cone, then the spaces were filled in with colored glazes (made by thinning and tinting the icing).

This decorating technique can be applied to any plain, smooth cookie. You can even dress up storebought graham crackers or tea biscuits. The patterns are limited only by your imagination. Look to folk art, fine art, and nature for inspiration.

To make royal icing, place 1 egg white in a deep mixing bowl. Gradually beat in 1 cup of confectioners' sugar and $\frac{1}{8}$ teaspoon of cream of tartar, then beat at high speed until the icing is creamy and quite stiff, 5 to 7 minutes. If you want to color the icing, add a small amount of food coloring and beat well. This recipe makes about $\frac{1}{2}$ cup, but it can be easily multiplied.

To make a glaze, transfer some royal icing to a small bowl. Stir in water, a few drops at a time, until the mixture is the consistency of white glue. Using a toothpick, add just a touch of food coloring to the glaze. Apply the glaze with small paintbrushes or cotton swabs.

Twist the top of the cone as you would a pastry bag, pushing the icing into the point. Make a separate cone for each color of icing you use.

The icing can now be piped in a very fine line. For thicker lines, snip off a portion of the cone's tip. The more you cut off, the thicker the line.

Pecan Lace Wafers

These crisp, filigreed lace cookies are so pretty, they practically create a party all by themselves. Make some of each type—wafers glazed with chocolate and rolled cones filled with whipped cream—and offer them on a tea tray. Or, serve the chocolate-glazed wafers with ice cream or sherbet in pretty, old-fashioned glass dishes. The cone-shaped, cream-filled cookies are delicious accompanied with raspberries or strawberries. Though not the easiest cookies to make, pecan lace wafers are worth the trouble. One helpful hint: be sure the baking sheet is cool before dropping the batter onto it.

While today we can buy nuts in many ready-to-use forms, this was not always so. Around the turn of the century, cooks relied on tips such as the following, from a popular household manual: "Pecan meats can be easily removed without breaking, by pouring boiling water over the nuts and letting them stand until cold. Then crack with a hammer, striking the small end of the pecan."

1 stick (4 ounces) butter, softened to
   room temperature
⅔ cup (packed) light brown sugar
½ cup light corn syrup
1 cup flour
1 cup finely chopped pecans
½ teaspoon vanilla extract

CHOCOLATE GLAZE
2 ounces semisweet chocolate
1 teaspoon vegetable shortening

WHIPPED CREAM FILLING
1 cup heavy cream
2 tablespoons confectioners' sugar

1. Preheat the oven to 375°. Lightly grease a baking sheet.

2. Cut the butter into 1-inch pieces. In a medium saucepan, heat the butter, brown sugar, and corn syrup over medium heat until the butter melts and the mixture comes to a boil. Remove the pan from the heat, add the flour, pecans, and vanilla extract, and stir until combined.

3. Using a teaspoonful of batter for each wafer, drop the batter onto the prepared baking sheet, leaving 3 inches of space between the wafers (bake no more than 9 at a time). Bake for 5 to 7 minutes, or until the wafers spread to about 2½ inches and the surface looks caramelized and lacy.

4. Let the wafers cool on the baking sheet for 20 to 30 seconds. To make cones, roll the wafers while they are still warm. (If the wafers cool before you have rolled them, return them to the oven for a moment to soften.) For flat cookies, transfer the wafers to a rack to cool completely.

5. Let the baking sheet cool, then make a second batch of wafers.

6. Meanwhile, make the chocolate glaze: In the top of a double boiler over hot, not simmering, water, melt the chocolate and vegetable shortening and stir until smooth; transfer the glaze to a bowl.

7. Drizzle the chocolate glaze from a spoon over the flat wafers, or carefully half-dip the wafers into the glaze. Dip just the edges of the cone-shaped wafers into the glaze.

8. Just before serving, make the filling: In a medium bowl, whip the cream with the confectioners' sugar until stiff. Spoon or pipe the sweetened whipped cream into the cone-shaped wafers.

Makes about 8 dozen

Pecan Lace Wafers

Lemon Squares with Jam Filling

Lemon Squares with Jam Filling

Rich but delicate, these cookies consist of a shortbread crust and lemon topping with a ribbon of jam sandwiched in between. If you've put up preserves, baking a batch of these cookies in midwinter would be a sweet and satisfying reminder of summer.

2 cups plus 3 tablespoons flour
⅓ cup confectioners' sugar, plus extra for dusting
¼ teaspoon salt
2 sticks (8 ounces) chilled butter, cut into pieces

1¼ cups granulated sugar
½ teaspoon baking powder
3 eggs
⅓ cup lemon juice
2 teaspoons grated lemon zest
¾ cup strawberry or raspberry jam

1. Preheat the oven to 350°. Grease and flour an 11 x 7-inch baking pan.
2. Make the crust: In a large bowl, stir together 2 cups of the flour, ⅓ cup of the

confectioners' sugar, and the salt. Using a pastry blender or two knives, cut in the butter until the mixture resembles coarse crumbs. Press the mixture into the prepared pan and bake for 15 minutes, or just until firm.

3. Meanwhile, make the lemon topping: In a medium bowl, stir together the granulated sugar, baking powder, and the remaining 3 tablespoons flour. Add the eggs, lemon juice, and lemon zest, and mix until well blended.

4. Remove the pan from the oven and spread the jam over the crust. Spread the lemon topping over the jam and bake for another 25 to 30 minutes, or until the topping is set.

5. Let cool in the pan on a rack. Dust the top lightly with confectioners' sugar before cutting into squares.

Makes 15 squares

Currant Griddle Cookies

Like the drop—or griddle—scone, a tradition at British country teas, these soft sesame-coated cookies are "baked" in a skillet on top of the stove. For a cozy tea, gather your guests in the kitchen and serve the cookies hot from the pan.

3½ cups flour

1 cup sugar

1 tablespoon baking powder

¾ teaspoon salt

1½ sticks (6 ounces) chilled butter, cut into pieces

4 tablespoons chilled vegetable shortening

1 cup dried currants

¾ cup sesame seeds

2 eggs

2 tablespoons milk

1 teaspoon vanilla extract

1. In a medium bowl, stir together the flour, sugar, baking powder, and salt.

2. Using a pastry blender or two knives, cut in the butter and vegetable shortening until the mixture resembles cornmeal. Stir in the currants and ¼ cup of the sesame seeds.

3. In a small bowl, beat the eggs, milk, and vanilla. Add the milk mixture to the flour mixture and stir until a cohesive dough forms.

4. Turn the dough out onto a lightly floured surface. Using a lightly floured rolling pin, roll the dough out to a ½-inch thickness. Cut out the cookies using a floured 2½-inch round cookie cutter. Gather, reroll, and cut any scraps. Sprinkle both sides of each cookie with some of the remaining ½ cup of sesame seeds and pat them gently into the dough.

5. Transfer the cookies to an ungreased baking sheet, cover with plastic wrap, and refrigerate for at least 2 hours.

6. Lightly oil a large nonstick skillet, then preheat it over medium-high heat. Place a few cookies at a time in the skillet and cook for 3 to 5 minutes on each side, or until the cookies are light golden brown. Serve the cookies warm, or reheat briefly in the oven before serving.

Makes about 2½ dozen

*I*n the early 1880s, it was reported that fashionable hostesses were making each cup of tea separately "in a perforated silver ball.... This is quite the prettiest way of making tea, and girls who appreciate the chance for coquetries and tableaux that the rite affords, are enamored with the tea ball, providing always that there is some gallant man about to handle the burning silver when it is necessary to empty and refill the ball."

Gingersnaps

For a crunchy topping, sprinkle these cookie-jar favorites with sugar while they are still warm. For a decorative design, use a drinking glass with a pressed or cut pattern, or a cookie stamp, to flatten the balls of dough.

2 cups flour
2 teaspoons ground ginger
1 teaspoon baking soda
¼ teaspoon salt
⅓ cup butter, softened to room
    temperature

⅓ cup vegetable shortening
1 cup (packed) dark brown sugar
1 egg
¼ cup molasses
2 tablespoons granulated sugar
    (optional)

BAKER'S
Best Chocolate
RECIPES

1. Preheat the oven to 350°. Lightly grease a baking sheet.

2. In a small bowl, stir together the flour, ginger, baking soda, and salt.

3. In a large bowl, cream the butter, shortening, and brown sugar. Add the egg, and beat until light and fluffy, about 3 minutes. Beat in the molasses. Gradually add the dry ingredients, beating well until the dough is smooth.

4. Shape the dough into 1-inch balls and place them on the prepared baking sheet, leaving 2 inches of space between them. Flatten them to a ¼-inch thickness by pressing them with the bottom of a glass dipped in cold water. Bake for 9 to 11 minutes, or until the cookies are slightly puffed.

5. Transfer the cookies to a rack and, if desired, sprinkle them with the granulated sugar while still warm.

Makes about 4½ dozen

Spritz Cookies

Cookies formed with a cookie press (which extrudes the dough through a patterned disk) are called *spritz*, the German word for "squirt." The buttery dough is usually flavored simply with vanilla, allowing the swirled shapes of the cookies to take center stage. A chocolate glaze and a dusting of chopped almonds add a finishing touch.

COOKIES
2 cups flour
½ teaspoon baking powder
2 sticks (8 ounces) butter, softened to
    room temperature
⅓ cup sugar
1 egg
½ teaspoon vanilla extract

GLAZE
3 ounces semisweet chocolate
4 teaspoons vegetable
    shortening
⅓ cup finely chopped blanched
    almonds

1. Preheat the oven to 350°. Lightly grease a baking sheet.

2. Make the cookies: In a small bowl, stir together the flour and baking powder.

In a large bowl, cream the butter and sugar until light and fluffy. Beat in the egg and vanilla. Gradually beat in the dry ingredients, beating well after each addition until the dough is smooth.

3. Fill a cookie press with the dough and form the cookies on the prepared baking sheet, leaving 1 inch of space between them. Bake for 11 to 13 minutes, or until the edges are just beginning to turn golden.

4. Let the cookies cool on the baking sheet for 2 to 3 minutes, then transfer them to a rack to cool completely before dipping them in the glaze.

5. Meanwhile, make the glaze: In the top of a double boiler over hot, not simmering, water, melt the chocolate and vegetable shortening and stir until smooth. Place the chopped almonds in a small bowl. Dip the cookies halfway into the glaze, then into the chopped almonds. Return the cookies to the rack until the glaze is set.

Makes about 3 dozen

Lemon Sugar Cookies

These are truly old-fashioned cookies: simple, crisp, and not overly sweet. Refrigerate the dough overnight—or for at least a few hours—so that it will be easier to handle and will require minimal flour for the rolling process.

2 cups flour
½ teaspoon baking soda
½ teaspoon cream of tartar
¼ teaspoon salt
1 stick (4 ounces) butter, softened to
  room temperature

1 teaspoon grated lemon zest
½ teaspoon vanilla extract
1 cup plus 2 tablespoons sugar
1 egg
2 tablespoons milk

1. In a small bowl, stir together the flour, baking soda, cream of tartar, and salt.

2. In a large bowl, cream the butter. Beat in the lemon zest and vanilla, then beat in 1 cup of the sugar. Beat in the egg and milk.

3. Gradually beat in the dry ingredients, beating well after each addition until the dough is smooth.

4. Turn the dough out onto a sheet of plastic wrap and form it into a ball. Wrap the dough and refrigerate it for at least 2 hours, or overnight.

5. Preheat the oven to 375°. Lightly grease a baking sheet.

6. Cut the dough into thirds; wrap two portions in plastic wrap and return them to the refrigerator. On a lightly floured surface, using a floured rolling pin, roll one portion of dough out to a ⅛-inch thickness.

7. Cut out the cookies using a floured 3-inch round cookie cutter. Gather, reroll, and cut any scraps. Transfer the cookies to the prepared baking sheet, leaving 1 inch of space between them. Bake for 10 to 12 minutes, or until the edges are just beginning to brown. Transfer the cookies to a rack and sprinkle them with the remaining 2 tablespoons sugar while still warm. Let the cookies cool completely.

8. Store the cookies in an airtight container.

Makes about 3 dozen

Two-Tone Icebox Cookies

Two-Tone Icebox Cookies

If you're in a hurry, this cookie dough can be frozen for forty-five minutes instead of refrigerated for four hours before baking. Or, the dough can be frozen for up to three months, then thawed in the refrigerator overnight before shaping.

2 sticks (8 ounces) butter, softened to
   room temperature
1 cup sugar
1 egg plus 1 egg yolk
1 teaspoon vanilla extract

2¾ cups flour
2 tablespoons unsweetened cocoa powder
1 egg white, beaten (optional)
Chopped or sliced blanched almonds
   (optional)

1. In a large bowl, cream the butter and sugar. Beat in the egg and egg yolk, then beat in the vanilla. Gradually add the flour, beating just until incorporated.

2. Divide the dough into two equal portions. Beat the cocoa into one portion. Form the dough into two balls. Use one of the techniques that follow to shape the cookies, then proceed with the baking directions in Steps 3 and 4.

For log cookies: Roll both the light and dark dough into ½-inch-thick ropes and cut the ropes into 2-inch lengths. Dip each log into beaten egg white, then into chopped or sliced almonds.

For checkerboard cookies (see the step-by-step photographs, pages 98-99): Using the dark dough, form ⅝-inch-diameter ropes about 9 inches long; form light-dough ropes the same size. Working with four ropes (two of each color) at a time, place one dark and one light rope side by side and press together; then place the other two ropes on top so that light and dark alternate; press together lightly. Wrap the dough loosely in plastic wrap and refrigerate for at least 4 hours, or overnight. Repeat with the remaining ropes. Remove one roll of dough at a time from the refrigerator and use a sharp knife to cut it into ¼-inch-thick slices.

For pinwheel cookies (see the step-by-step photographs, pages 98-99): Divide each ball of dough into eight equal portions, then roll each out to a 6 x 5-inch rectangle. Place a dark piece of dough on top of a light one (or vice versa) and roll the two layers together tightly from one long side, like a jelly roll. Wrap each roll in plastic wrap and refrigerate for at least 4 hours. Use a sharp knife to cut the dough into ¼-inch-thick slices.

3. Preheat the oven to 350°. Lightly grease a baking sheet.

4. Place the cookies on the prepared baking sheet, leaving 1 inch of space between the cookies, and bake for 8 to 10 minutes for checkerboard or pinwheel cookies and 11 to 13 minutes for log cookies, or until they are lightly browned around the edges.

5. Cool the cookies on a rack.

Makes 8 to 12 dozen

DESIGNS FOR TWO-TONE ICEBOX COOKIES

CHECKERBOARD

Two-Tone Icebox Cookies (page 96) can be designed in any number of ways. One of the simpler patterns is the checkerboard, which is formed by alternating ropes of light and dark dough. The size of the cookies can be varied by making the diameter of the ropes larger or smaller, but the cookies should not be sliced any thicker than ¼ inch. If desired, the cookie log can be patted into a slightly squarer shape.

Divide the light and dark portions of dough into eight pieces each. Roll each piece into a rope ⅝ inch in diameter and about 9 inches long, for a total of 16 ropes.

Working with four ropes (two of each color) at a time, press a light-dough rope and a dark-dough rope together. Repeat with the other two ropes.

BULL'S-EYE

To make bull's-eye cookies, wrap a dough rectangle of one color around a dough log of contrasting color. Make half the cookies with dark-dough centers and half with light-dough centers. If desired, you can use this same technique to give the checkerboard pattern (above) a border: simply roll out some of the dough to a rectangle ⅛ inch thick and big enough to wrap around the checkerboard cookie roll.

Divide the light and dark portions of dough into four pieces each. Roll two pieces of each color into 6 x 4-inch rectangles; roll two pieces of each color into 6-inch logs.

There should be two rectangles and two logs of each color. Place a log of dough about ½ inch in from the long side of a rectangle of dough of contrasting color.

PINWHEEL

To make pinwheel cookies, layer two rectangles of different-colored dough together, then roll them up. For a colorful variation on this theme, instead of using the chocolate and vanilla doughs shown here, add two different food colors to the plain dough: Try red-and-green pinwheels for Christmas. Or, for Halloween, use cocoa to make chocolate dough and color the other portion of dough a pale orange.

Divide the light and dark portions of dough into four pieces each, for a total of eight pieces. Roll each piece into a 6 x 5-inch rectangle about ⅛ inch thick.

Place one rectangle of dough on top of another rectangle of contrasting color. It doesn't matter which color is on top. There should be four pairs of rectangles.

Place one pair of ropes on top of the other, alternating light and dark doughs. Press the ropes together to form a long roll. Repeat with the remaining dough.

Wrap each cookie roll in plastic wrap and refrigerate for at least 4 hours, or overnight, to firm up. When ready to bake, slice the roll into ¼-inch-thick cookies.

To bake, place the cookies 1 inch apart on a lightly greased baking sheet and bake at 350° for 8 to 10 minutes, or until lightly browned around the edges.

Roll up the log in the rectangle of dough. Pinch the ends of the dough rectangle together to completely enclose the log and press the seam lightly to smooth it.

Wrap each cookie roll in plastic wrap and refrigerate for at least 4 hours, or overnight, to firm up. When ready to bake, slice the roll into ¼-inch-thick cookies.

To bake, place the cookies 1 inch apart on a lightly greased baking sheet and bake at 350° for 8 to 10 minutes, or until lightly browned around the edges.

Starting at one long side, tightly roll up the layered dough. Pinch the ends of the rectangles together to seal, then press lightly to smooth the seam against the log.

Wrap each cookie roll in plastic wrap and refrigerate for at least 4 hours, or overnight, to firm up. When ready to bake, slice the roll into ¼-inch-thick cookies.

To bake, place the cookies 1 inch apart on a lightly greased baking sheet and bake at 350° for 8 to 10 minutes, or until lightly browned around the edges.

Brownie Cheesecake Bars

America's longtime love affair with brownies and cheesecake has led, happily and perhaps inevitably, to this satisfying combination of the two: a creamy layer of cheese-cake "frosting" sits atop a light chocolate brownie base.

BROWNIE LAYER

1 cup flour

⅓ cup unsweetened cocoa powder

1 teaspoon baking powder

4 tablespoons butter, softened to room temperature

⅓ cup sugar

2 eggs

¼ cup milk

CREAM CHEESE LAYER

1 package (8 ounces) cream cheese, softened to room temperature

¼ cup sugar

1 egg, lightly beaten

⅓ cup sour cream

½ teaspoon vanilla extract

⅔ cup sliced unblanched almonds

1. Preheat the oven to 350°. Grease an 8-inch square pan, line it with a square of greased waxed paper, then flour the pan.

2. Make the brownie layer: In a small bowl, stir together the flour, cocoa powder, and baking powder.

3. In a large bowl, cream the butter and sugar. Beat in the eggs, one at a time, beating well after each addition. Alternating between the two, add the dry ingredients and the milk, beating well after each addition.

4. Spread the batter evenly in the prepared pan. Rap the pan once or twice on the counter to remove any air pockets. Bake for 10 minutes, or until the brownie layer is just set.

5. Meanwhile, make the cream cheese layer: In a medium bowl, beat the cream cheese and sugar until smooth. Beat in the egg, sour cream, and vanilla.

6. Pour the cream cheese mixture evenly over the brownie layer, spreading it with a rubber spatula. Sprinkle the almonds evenly over the cream cheese layer and bake for another 20 to 25 minutes, or until the cream cheese layer is set.

7. Let cool completely in the pan on a rack, then cut into 15 bars.   *Makes 15*

New York-style cheesecake, based on Eastern European recipes, is a firm, dense cake, made by blending cream cheese, cottage cheese, or farmer cheese with sweet or sour cream. It is most often flavored with vanilla and/or lemon. Italian cheesecake, derived from recipes for torta di ricotta, has a pastry crust; its ricotta-cheese filling is studded with candied fruit and almonds, and flavored with Marsala wine or liqueur.

Brownie Cheesecake Bars

Dream Bars

Even though this rich cookie has numerous variations, most recipes call for a buttery crust and a chewy topping of nuts and coconut. Perhaps the ultimate bar cookie, these should satisfy any cookie lover's dreams.

CRUST
1 cup flour
¼ cup (packed) dark brown sugar
1 stick (4 ounces) chilled butter, cut into pieces

COCONUT-PECAN TOPPING
1 cup sweetened shredded coconut
1 cup coarsely chopped pecans

2 tablespoons flour
¾ teaspoon baking powder
¼ teaspoon salt
2 eggs
¾ cup (packed) dark brown sugar
1 teaspoon vanilla extract
1 teaspoon grated lemon zest

1. Preheat the oven to 375°. Grease and flour an 11 x 7-inch baking pan.
2. Make the crust: In a medium bowl, stir together the flour and brown sugar. Using your fingers or a fork, mix in the butter until the mixture resembles very coarse crumbs. Press the mixture into the prepared pan and bake for 10 minutes.
3. Meanwhile, make the coconut-pecan topping: In a small bowl, combine the coconut, pecans, flour, baking powder, and salt.
4. In a medium bowl, beat together the eggs, brown sugar, vanilla, and lemon zest. Stir the dry ingredients into the egg mixture.
5. Remove the pan from the oven and let the crust cool slightly. Pour the coconut-pecan topping over the crust, spreading it evenly with a rubber spatula, and bake for another 18 to 20 minutes, or until the topping is golden brown and set.
6. Let cool slightly in the pan on a rack, then cut into 20 bars while still warm.

Makes 20

Benne Wafers

Benne (sesame seed) cookies have been a Southern specialty—particularly associated with Charleston, South Carolina—since the days when sesame seeds were brought over from Africa on slave ships. These thin, chewy wafers are loaded with toasted sesame seeds. Toasting the seeds, like toasting nuts, brings out their full flavor.

1 cup sesame seeds
¾ cup flour
¼ teaspoon baking powder
1 stick (4 ounces) butter, softened to
  room temperature

1 cup (packed) light brown sugar
1 egg
1 teaspoon vanilla extract

1. In an ungreased, heavy skillet, toast the sesame seeds over low heat, stirring constantly, until light golden, 5 to 7 minutes. Set aside to cool.

2. In a small bowl, stir together the flour and baking powder.

3. In a medium bowl, cream the butter and sugar. Beat in the egg. Beat in the dry ingredients, then add the toasted sesame seeds and the vanilla, and stir until combined.

4. Transfer the dough to a sheet of waxed paper or plastic wrap and shape it into a log about 1½ inches thick. Wrap the log of dough and refrigerate it overnight.

5. Preheat the oven to 350°. Grease a large baking sheet.

6. Using a very sharp knife, cut the dough into ⅛-inch-thick slices and place them on the prepared baking sheet, leaving 3 to 4 inches of space between them. Bake for 8 to 10 minutes, or until the edges are lightly browned.

7. Let the wafers cool for about 30 seconds on the baking sheet, then, using a thin metal spatula and wiping it clean periodically, transfer them to a rack to cool completely.

Makes about 6 dozen

Pecan Balls

Although a wonderful treat any time of the year, these dense, sugar-dusted cookies are traditionally baked at Christmas. They do make attractive holiday gifts, especially when placed in individual foil bonbon cups and set in decorative tins.

1½ cups pecan halves
1 stick (4 ounces) butter, softened to
 room temperature
¼ cup granulated sugar

2 teaspoons vanilla extract
2 cups flour
¼ cup confectioners' sugar

1. Preheat the oven to 300°. Lightly grease a baking sheet.

2. Place the pecans in an ungreased, heavy skillet. Toast them over medium-high heat, shaking the pan frequently, until golden brown, 5 to 8 minutes.

3. Process the pecans in a food processor or blender just until finely chopped; do not overprocess or the nuts will turn into an oily paste. Set aside.

4. In a large bowl, cream the butter and granulated sugar until light and fluffy. Beat in the vanilla. Beat in the chopped pecans. Gradually add the flour, beating until just incorporated. The dough will be firm and slightly crumbly.

5. Shape the dough into 1-inch balls and place them on the prepared baking sheet, leaving 1 inch of space between them. Bake for 18 to 20 minutes, or until the cookies just begin to brown around the sides. The tops should remain pale.

6. Let the cookies cool on the baking sheet for 5 minutes, then carefully transfer them to a rack. While they are still warm, sift the confectioners' sugar over them, then let them cool completely.

Makes about 3½ dozen

Oatmeal Chocolate-Chunk Cookies

These large cookies are filled with suitably oversized chunks of chocolate—just as the original chocolate-chip cookies were before packaged chips were sold. The chocolate will cut more cleanly if it is slightly warmer than room temperature.

1⅓ cups flour
1 teaspoon baking soda
½ teaspoon salt
2 sticks (8 ounces) butter, softened to
   room temperature
¼ cup vegetable shortening
¾ cup (packed) dark brown sugar

⅓ cup granulated sugar
1 egg
1 teaspoon vanilla extract
3 cups old-fashioned rolled oats
6 ounces semisweet chocolate, cut into
   coarse chunks
1 cup coarsely chopped unblanched almonds

1. Preheat the oven to 375°. Lightly grease a baking sheet.

2. In a small bowl, stir together the flour, baking soda, and salt.

3. In a large bowl, cream the butter, shortening, and sugars until light and fluffy. Beat in the egg and vanilla. Gradually add the dry ingredients, stirring just until incorporated. Stir in the oats, chocolate chunks, and almonds.

4. Drop ¼-cup portions of the cookie dough onto the prepared baking sheet, leaving 3 to 4 inches of space between the cookies. Flatten each portion of dough slightly with your fingertips. Bake for 13 to 15 minutes, or until the cookies are lightly browned on the edges.

5. Let the cookies cool on the baking sheet for 2 to 3 minutes, then transfer them to a rack to cool completely.

Makes about 2 dozen

A 1924 children's cookbook captured the importance of the cookie jar: " 'Have you a cooky-jar?' I asked Ellen as I wrapped up a dozen nice fresh oatmeal cookies for her. It was just as I suspected—they didn't have one, and while mother says a cooky-jar in a house with eleven children in it would be empty most of the time—I intend to try to help Ellen get one. Home wouldn't seem home to me without a cooky-jar. . . ."

Auntie Rae's Apple Bars

The top crust of these bars is created by an unusual method: dough is grated into thick shreds, which bake into a crunchy crust sparkling with cinnamon-sugar. Add a little lemon zest or vanilla extract to the apples if they are not flavorful enough.

6 Granny Smith or other tart apples
   (about 2½ pounds)
2 tablespoons lemon juice
4 cups flour
1 teaspoon baking powder
½ teaspoon baking soda

1¼ cups sugar
½ cup vegetable oil
2 eggs
1½ teaspoons vanilla extract
1 tablespoon cinnamon

1. Preheat the oven to 350° Grease and flour a 13 x 9-inch baking pan.

2. Peel and coarsely grate the apples. Place them in a large bowl and toss them with the lemon juice, then set aside in a colander to drain.

3. In a medium bowl, stir together the flour, baking powder, and baking soda.

Oatmeal Chocolate-Chunk Cookies

4. In a large bowl, beat together ¾ cup of the sugar and the oil. Beat in the eggs, one at a time, beating well until light. Beat in the vanilla. Gradually add the dry ingredients, mixing well after each addition. The dough should be very stiff; add a little more flour if it does not seem stiff enough to grate.

5. Divide the dough into two equal portions. Press half of the dough evenly into the bottom of the prepared pan. Pat the grated apples dry with paper towels, then spread them evenly over the bottom layer of dough.

6. In a small bowl, stir together the remaining ½ cup sugar and the cinnamon. Sprinkle the apples with half of the cinnamon sugar.

7. Using the coarse side of a grater, grate the remaining dough over the apples, covering them as completely as possible; do not press or flatten the dough. Sprinkle the remaining cinnamon sugar over the topping and bake for 55 to 60 minutes, or until the topping is crisp and golden.

8. Let cool in the pan on a rack, then cut into 20 large bars. Serve warm. If not serving immediately, reheat briefly before serving to crisp the topping.   *Makes 20*

COOKIE JARS

The ancestors of the delightful cookie jars that brighten our kitchens were the stoneware crocks used for centuries in American homes. Cookies were stored in "stone jars" to preserve their freshness.

In the 1920s, inspired perhaps by the china "biscuit jars" of Victorian England, American art potteries began to produce hand-painted cookie jars in limited editions. By the 1930s, however, colorful mass-produced jars, durably glazed for everyday use, were staples of firms such as Ohio's McCoy Pottery Company.

Today, collectors of old cookie jars can find plentiful "pickings" at antique shows, flea markets, and tag sales. Although the early limited editions are eagerly sought by some, it is the playful jars from the 1940s through the 1960s, still relatively inexpensive, that seem to attract the majority of cookie-jar lovers.

Keep an eye on condition when buying a cookie jar, as cracks and chips will lessen its value. Also, beware of reproductions. Although some old jars bear maker's marks, many do not. One way to distinguish an old piece is by its weight: new imports are lighter than old American jars. Finally, check the fit and color match to determine whether the bottom and top belong together. "Married" cookie jars are less desirable than those that were "made for each other."

For a collecting challenge, seek out all the variations of one model, such as the McCoy apple-topped basket (bottom left), which was also made with pear, banana, pine-cone, and puppy lids.

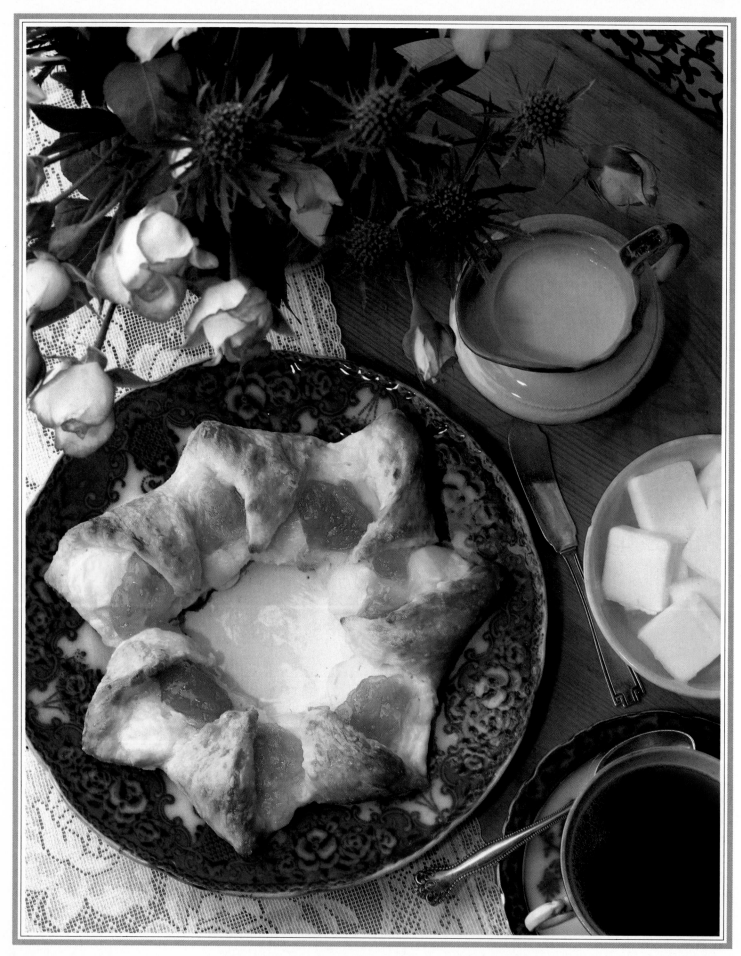

Quick Breads, Coffee Cakes, and Muffins

for breakfast, tea, and snacks

Their very name makes them sound like a modern invention, but quick breads include such old-fashioned favorites as soda bread and johnnycake. It is precisely because they are so easy to prepare that such breads make the perfect solution for last-minute entertaining. What better way to impress unexpected guests than with a delicate lemon bread or date-nut loaf baked in their presence?

Muffins, too, can be made with a minimum of effort. Indeed, much of their charm—aside from their tantalizing flavor—lies in the speed with which they go from mixing bowl to table. On the following pages you will find recipes for such breakfast classics as blueberry, apple, and banana muffins, as well as for a savory dinner muffin flavored with chiles and cheese.

And though coffee cakes do take a bit longer to make, the ones you prepare yourself will far surpass the store-bought varieties. Try a blueberry-topped cake, a cheese-filled ring, or a pretty apple pastry. Then put on the coffee pot and call the neighbors.

Start a Saturday by having friends over for Apricot-Cheese Coffee Ring.

Blueberry Coffee Cake

Juicy, naturally sweet blueberries don't need much enhancement—the simplest recipes display them beautifully. This recipe is quick to mix, but takes a little longer than most cakes to bake—all the more time to fill the house with its enticing fragrance. If your schedule doesn't allow for weekday coffee klatches, bake this cake for a casual Saturday afternoon gathering or a convivial Sunday brunch.

B*efore the invention of double-acting baking powder, a cook had to be something of a chemist: when baking soda was used as the sole leavening agent, an acid ingredient was needed to activate the soda. In the days of home-churned butter, buttermilk was often on hand; or soured milk (sometimes called "loppered" milk) served the purpose. Today, sweet milk soured with vinegar or lemon juice can take the place of buttermilk.*

CAKE LAYER
1 cup flour
1 teaspoon baking powder
½ teaspoon baking soda
¼ teaspoon salt
1 stick (4 ounces) butter, softened to
   room temperature
⅔ cup (packed) light brown sugar
1 egg
¼ cup buttermilk, or ¼ cup milk
   plus ¾ teaspoon vinegar
1 teaspoon vanilla extract

TOPPING AND FILLING
¼ cup flour
½ teaspoon cinnamon
3 tablespoons chilled butter, cut into
   pieces
3 cups (about 1½ pints) blueberries
2 teaspoons confectioners' sugar

1. Preheat the oven to 350°. Butter an 8-inch round cake pan and line the bottom with waxed paper. Butter the waxed paper, then flour the pan.

2. Make the cake layer: In a medium bowl, stir together the flour, baking powder, baking soda, and salt.

3. In a large bowl, cream the butter and brown sugar. Beat in the egg, buttermilk, and vanilla. Gradually add the dry ingredients, beating well after each addition. Spread the batter evenly in the prepared pan; set aside.

4. Make the topping: In a small bowl, mix the flour and cinnamon. Using a pastry blender or two knives, cut in the butter until the mixture resembles coarse crumbs.

5. Spread the blueberries evenly over the cake layer, then sprinkle the topping over them. Bake for 1 hour to 1 hour and 10 minutes, or until the topping is golden and beginning to brown around the edges.

6. Let the cake cool in the pan on a rack for 30 minutes.

7. Run the tip of a knife around the edge of the pan to loosen the cake, then turn it out onto a plate. Immediately invert the cake onto a serving plate. Dust the top with the confectioners' sugar and serve warm.

Makes one 8-inch cake

Blueberry Coffee Cake

Ginger-Carrot Muffins

The sharpness of fresh ginger and the sweetness of ground ginger combine to give these muffins a tantalizing flavor equally welcome at breakfast or snack time. If you don't use fresh ginger very often, buy the smallest piece available; wrap it tightly in plastic wrap and keep it in the freezer. The ginger need not be thawed before grating; in fact, it grates more easily when frozen.

2 cups flour
1 cup (packed) dark brown sugar
1 teaspoon baking powder
1 teaspoon baking soda
¼ teaspoon ground ginger
¼ teaspoon salt
2 eggs, lightly beaten

½ cup sour cream
½ cup vegetable oil
2 cups grated carrots (about 2 large)
¼ cup golden raisins
¼ cup coarsely chopped walnuts
2 tablespoons grated fresh ginger

1. Preheat the oven to 425°. Butter and flour 12 muffin tin cups, or line them with paper baking cups.
2. In a large bowl, stir together the flour, sugar, baking powder, baking soda, ground ginger, and salt.
3. In a small bowl, combine the eggs, sour cream, and oil, and mix until blended. Pour the egg mixture into the dry ingredients and stir just until blended. Add the carrots, raisins, walnuts, and fresh ginger, and stir just until combined; do not overmix.
4. Divide the batter evenly among the prepared muffin tin cups and bake for 15 to 20 minutes, or until the tops of the muffins are golden and a toothpick inserted in the center of a muffin comes out clean and dry. *Makes 1 dozen*

Lemon Tea Loaf

The ingredients for this delicate tea bread are ones you are likely to have on hand—a lifesaver when company's coming on short notice. There is a special satisfaction in greeting friends with a steaming pot of tea and freshly baked bread.

2 large lemons
2 cups flour
2 teaspoons baking powder
½ teaspoon baking soda
½ teaspoon salt

2 sticks (8 ounces) butter, softened to
*   room temperature*
¾ cup sugar
3 eggs

1. Preheat the oven to 350°. Butter and flour a 9 x 5-inch loaf pan.
2. Grate enough zest from the lemons to measure 2 teaspoons, then squeeze enough juice to measure ¼ cup; set aside.

3. In a medium bowl, stir together the flour, baking powder, baking soda, and salt; set aside.

4. In a large bowl, cream the butter and sugar. Beat in the eggs, one at a time, beating well after each addition. Beat in the lemon zest and juice. Gradually add the dry ingredients, stirring just until incorporated.

5. Spread the batter evenly in the prepared pan. Rap the pan once or twice on the counter to remove any air pockets. Bake for 55 to 60 minutes, or until the top of the loaf is golden, the bread shrinks from the sides of the pan, and a toothpick inserted in the center comes out clean and dry.

6. Let the loaf cool in the pan on a rack, then turn it out to cool completely before slicing.

Makes one 9-inch loaf

Pineapple Macadamia Muffins

Fresh pineapple tastes best in this recipe, but canned pineapple can be substituted. The creamy, delicate flavor of macadamia nuts adds a luxurious touch to the muffins. Macadamias, always sold shelled, are more perishable than most other nuts, so keep them in the freezer until needed.

1 small fresh pineapple, or 1 cup drained,
  crushed canned pineapple
2 cups flour
¾ cup sugar
1 tablespoon baking powder
1 teaspoon baking soda
½ teaspoon salt

3 eggs, lightly beaten
¼ cup buttermilk, or ¼ cup milk plus
  ¾ teaspoon vinegar
⅓ cup butter, melted
2 teaspoons vanilla extract
1 tablespoon grated lemon or lime zest
½ cup coarsely chopped macadamia nuts

1. Preheat the oven to 400°. Butter and flour 6 large (3½-inch) muffin tin cups (or 15 regular-size cups), or line them with paper baking cups.

2. Prepare the pineapple: Using a large, heavy knife, cut off the leafy top. Quarter the pineapple lengthwise, then remove the rind, eyes, and core from each wedge. Finely chop enough pineapple to measure 1 cup; reserve the remaining pineapple for another use.

3. In a large bowl, stir together the flour, sugar, baking powder, baking soda, and salt, and make a well in the center.

4. In a small bowl, stir together the eggs, buttermilk, butter, vanilla, and lemon zest. Pour the egg mixture into the dry ingredients and stir just until blended. Add the chopped pineapple and stir just until combined; do not overmix. Stir in the macadamia nuts.

5. Divide the batter evenly among the prepared muffin tin cups and bake for 20 to 25 minutes (check regular-size muffins after 15 minutes), or until the muffins are golden and cracked on top, and a toothpick inserted in the center of a muffin comes out clean and dry. Serve warm.

Makes 6 large or 15 regular-size muffins

Maple Cornsticks

Maple Cornsticks

Sweetened with pure maple syrup, these cornsticks are a treat served hot for breakfast. Standard or miniature muffin tins can be used instead of a cornstick pan.

1 cup flour	*1 cup buttermilk, or 1 cup milk plus*
1 cup yellow cornmeal	*1 tablespoon vinegar*
2 teaspoons baking powder	*⅓ cup maple syrup*
½ teaspoon baking soda	*1 cup fresh corn kernels (about 2 ears),*
½ teaspoon salt	*or 1 cup frozen corn kernels, thawed*
2 eggs	*3 tablespoons butter, melted*

1. Preheat the oven to 425°. Grease a cornstick pan.

2. In a small bowl, stir together the flour, cornmeal, baking powder, baking soda, and salt.

3. In a large bowl, beat the eggs until foamy. Beat in the buttermilk and maple syrup, then stir in the corn. Gradually add the dry ingredients, beating well after each addition. Stir in the butter.

4. Pour the batter into the prepared pan, filling each mold about three-quarters full, and smooth the surface of the batter with a rubber spatula. Bake for 15 to 18 minutes, or until the sticks shrink from the sides of the pan and the tops are golden brown. Serve hot. *Makes 2 dozen*

Banana Oat Bran Muffins

Health-conscious Americans have made bran muffins increasingly popular. These are made with oat bran, which has a more delicate flavor and texture than wheat bran.

1½ cups flour
½ cup oat bran
½ cup (packed) dark brown sugar
1 teaspoon baking powder
½ teaspoon baking soda
¼ teaspoon salt

1 egg, lightly beaten
1 ripe banana, mashed (about ½ cup)
½ cup vegetable oil
¼ cup buttermilk, or ¼ cup milk plus
  ¾ teaspoon vinegar

1. Preheat the oven to 400°. Butter and flour 12 muffin tin cups, or line them with paper baking cups.

2. In a large bowl, stir together the flour, oat bran, sugar, baking powder, baking soda, and salt, and make a well in the center.

3. In a medium bowl, stir together the egg, banana, oil, and buttermilk. Pour the egg mixture into the dry ingredients and stir just until blended; do not overmix.

4. Divide the batter evenly among the prepared muffin tin cups and bake for 18 to 20 minutes, or until the tops of the muffins are golden and a toothpick inserted in the center of a muffin comes out clean and dry.   *Makes 1 dozen*

Pumpkin Corn Muffins

The mellow sweetness of these golden-orange muffins pairs equally well with jam at breakfast, or with soups and savory main dishes at lunch or dinner.

1 cup flour
¾ cup yellow cornmeal
1 teaspoon baking powder
½ teaspoon baking soda
¼ teaspoon salt

2 eggs, well beaten
1 cup canned unsweetened pumpkin
½ cup (packed) dark brown sugar
4 tablespoons butter, melted
1 cup coarsely chopped pecans

1. Preheat the oven to 425°. Butter and flour 12 muffin tin cups, or line them with paper baking cups.

2. In a large bowl, stir together the flour, cornmeal, baking powder, baking soda, and salt, and make a well in the center.

3. In a small bowl, stir together the eggs, pumpkin, sugar, and butter. Pour the egg mixture into the dry ingredients and mix just until blended; do not overmix. Add the pecans, and stir just until combined.

4. Divide the batter evenly among the prepared muffin tin cups and bake for 15 to 18 minutes, or until the tops of the muffins are golden and a toothpick inserted in the center of a muffin comes out clean and dry.   *Makes 1 dozen*

There is a marked difference between the cornmeal ground at the South, and that which is sent out from Northern mills," noted Marion Harland in 1871 in Common Sense in the Household. *"Moreover, there is a partiality at the North for yellow meal, which the Southerners regard as only fit for chicken and cattle-feed."*

MUFFIN PANS

Before the middle of the 19th century, cooks used patty pans (small pie tins), stoneware cups, or individual metal molds for baking diminutive breads, rolls, cakes, and biscuits. One of the first multi-unit joined pans, forerunner of today's muffin tins, was patented in 1859.

By the late 1800s, American cookbooks included recipes for "gems" —small muffins and rolls—which were to be baked in "gem pans," very much like modern muffin pans. In 1893, *Miss Parloa's Young Housekeeper* included "muffin pans, two—each holding eight or twelve muffins" in a list of kitchen "articles most in use."

The earliest joined muffin pans were sets of small cups connected with a heavy wire or a soldered strip of tin. These "cut and pieced" pans were succeeded by those made of stamped tin; cast-iron and tinned-iron pans came later. Griswold, a cookware company located in Erie, Pennsylvania, was one of the first American producers of cast-iron pans; today, Griswold products remain popular with kitchenware collectors. Surprisingly, cast-iron corn-stick pans (which turn out breads shaped like ears of corn) are a relatively recent invention; although they may have existed by 1900, they were not patented until 1920.

In the collection displayed here, antique and contemporary pans of iron, tin, and aluminum show a remarkable variety of pattern and form. With proper care, old pans can be used to turn out muffins and corn-sticks that recall an earlier era.

Currant-Pecan Sticky Buns

Philadelphia is famous for these spicy swirls of dough; they are usually called "cinnamon buns" in that city, where they have been popular since the 19th century.

1 cup milk
2 sticks (8 ounces) butter, softened to
  room temperature
⅓ cup granulated sugar
¼ cup lukewarm (105° to 115°) water
1 package active dry yeast
About 5¼ cups flour

½ teaspoon salt
1 egg, lightly beaten
1⅓ cups coarsely chopped pecans
1¼ cups (packed) dark brown sugar
⅔ cup dried currants
1 tablespoon cinnamon
½ cup dark corn syrup

1. In a small saucepan, scald the milk over medium heat. Add 4 tablespoons of the butter and the granulated sugar, and stir until the butter is melted and the sugar is dissolved. Set the mixture aside to cool to lukewarm (105° to 115°).

2. Place the water in a small bowl and sprinkle the yeast over it. Stir in a pinch of granulated sugar and let stand until the yeast begins to foam, about 5 minutes.

3. In a large bowl, stir together 4¾ cups of the flour and the salt, and make a well in the center. Pour in the milk mixture, the yeast mixture, and the egg, and stir until the mixture forms a soft dough.

4. Transfer the dough to a lightly floured surface and knead it until smooth and elastic, 5 to 10 minutes, adding up to ½ cup more flour, if necessary, to keep the dough from sticking. Form the dough into a ball and place it in a large greased bowl. Cover the bowl with a slightly dampened kitchen towel, set it aside in a warm, draft-free place, and let the dough rise until it doubles in bulk, 45 minutes to 1 hour.

5. Meanwhile, lightly butter two 9-inch cake pans.

6. In a small bowl, stir together ⅔ cup of the pecans, ¾ cup of the brown sugar, the currants, and cinnamon; set the currant-pecan filling aside.

7. For the glaze: In a heavy saucepan, combine the corn syrup, 1 stick of the butter, and the remaining ⅔ cup pecans and ½ cup brown sugar. Cook over low heat, stirring constantly, until the butter is melted and the sugar is dissolved. Dividing it evenly, pour the glaze into the bottoms of the prepared cake pans.

8. Punch the dough down, then transfer it to a lightly floured surface. Using a lightly floured rolling pin, roll out the dough to a 12 x 21-inch rectangle about ¼ inch thick. Brush the dough with the remaining 4 tablespoons butter, then sprinkle it with the currant-pecan filling.

9. Starting at one long side, roll the dough jelly-roll fashion. Cut the roll into fourteen 1½-inch slices. Place 6 slices, cut-side down, in a circle around the edge of each glaze-filled cake pan and one in the center of each. Set aside, uncovered, in a warm, draft-free place, and let rise until the dough doubles in bulk, about 25 minutes.

10. Preheat the oven to 375°. Bake for 25 to 30 minutes, or until the buns are golden brown. Immediately run the tip of a knife around the edges of the pans, then carefully invert the buns onto serving platters. Serve warm. *Makes 14 buns*

Currant-Pecan Sticky Buns

Buttermilk Scones with Raisins

The British tea breads known as scones, which might be described as a cross between rich biscuits and muffins, have been wholeheartedly adopted by Americans. Serve scones hot from the oven, with sweet butter and a selection of jams and marmalades. If there are any left over, reheat them before serving.

3⅓ cups flour
3 tablespoons sugar
1 tablespoon baking powder
¼ teaspoon salt
3 eggs, lightly beaten

¾ cup buttermilk
1 stick (4 ounces) chilled butter, cut
*   into pieces*
½ cup golden raisins
½ cup coarsely chopped walnuts

1. Preheat the oven to 425°. Lightly grease a large baking sheet.
2. In a large bowl, stir together the flour, sugar, baking powder, and salt.
3. Set aside 2 tablespoons of the beaten eggs for glazing the scones. In a small bowl, stir together the remaining eggs and the buttermilk; set aside.
4. Using a pastry blender or two knives, cut the butter into the dry ingredients until the mixture resembles coarse crumbs. Stir in the raisins and walnuts, and make a well in the center.

Buttermilk Scones with Raisins

5. Pour in the egg mixture and stir just until blended. Continue stirring the mixture until it forms a dough that can be gathered into a ball.

6. Place the dough on a lightly floured surface and knead it until smooth, 3 to 5 minutes. Using a lightly floured rolling pin, roll out the dough to a ¾-inch-thick round, 9 to 10 inches in diameter.

7. Using a sharp knife dipped in flour, cut the dough into 12 wedges. Transfer the wedges to the prepared baking sheet and brush the tops and the cut edges with the reserved beaten egg. Bake for 18 to 20 minutes, or until the scones are puffed and golden brown. Serve hot.

Makes 1 dozen

Triple Almond Coffee Cake

A crunchy topping of chopped almonds enhances this rich cake flavored with both almond paste and almond extract. Made from ground almonds and sugar, almond paste can be found in the imported food section of many supermarkets.

CAKE LAYER
1¾ cups flour
1 teaspoon baking powder
½ teaspoon baking soda
½ teaspoon salt
2 sticks (8 ounces) butter, softened to
    room temperature
1 package (8 ounces) almond paste
2 tablespoons granulated sugar
2 eggs

½ teaspoon almond extract
¾ cup buttermilk, or ¾ cup milk
    plus 2¼ teaspoons vinegar

TOPPING
⅓ cup (packed) light brown sugar
¼ cup flour
4 tablespoons chilled butter, cut into
    pieces
¾ cup coarsely chopped almonds

1. Preheat the oven to 350°. Butter and flour a 9-inch square baking pan.

2. Make the cake layer: In a medium bowl, stir together the flour, baking powder, baking soda, and salt.

3. In a large bowl, cream the butter and almond paste. Beat in the granulated sugar, then add the eggs, one at a time, beating well after each addition. Blend in the almond extract.

4. Alternating between the two, add the dry ingredients and the buttermilk, beating just until incorporated. Spread the batter evenly in the prepared pan; set aside.

5. Make the topping: In a small bowl, stir together the brown sugar and flour. Using a pastry blender or two knives, cut in the butter until the mixture resembles coarse crumbs. Stir in the almonds.

6. Sprinkle the topping over the batter and bake for 40 to 45 minutes, or until the cake shrinks from the sides of the pan and a toothpick inserted into the center of the cake comes out clean and dry.

7. Let the cake cool in the pan on a rack for about 15 minutes, then cut it into squares.

Makes one 9-inch square cake

Mrs. Hill's New Cook Book, *published in 1870, offered detailed directions for making coffee: "Procure a percolator; take out all the inside machinery; scald it; allow four ounces of ground coffee to a quart of water . . . add a small piece of isinglass or skin of cod fish (these answer for clarifying when eggs are scarce) . . . pour in boiling water; set the percolator where it will keep hot without boiling . . . pour a little into a cup, and, if not satisfactorily strong, . . . let it drip through the second time."*

Blueberry Muffins with Almonds

Every expert country cook needs a good blueberry muffin recipe, and since muffin-making is quite simple, this one might also be a good starting point for teaching children to bake. In summer, the lesson could begin with a trip to a pick-your-own berry farm—an inspiring start for young bakers. Bring home some extra berries to freeze, or bake an extra batch of muffins and freeze them for winter mornings.

2 cups flour

½ cup plus 1 tablespoon sugar

2 teaspoons baking powder

½ teaspoon baking soda

¼ teaspoon salt

1 egg, lightly beaten

1 cup milk

4 tablespoons butter, melted

1 cup blueberries

½ cup coarsely chopped almonds

2 teaspoons grated orange zest

1. Preheat the oven to 425°. Butter and flour 12 muffin tin cups, or line them with paper baking cups.

2. In a large bowl, stir together the flour, ½ cup of the sugar, the baking powder, baking soda, and salt, and make a well in the center.

3. In a small bowl, stir together the egg, milk, and butter. Pour the egg mixture into the dry ingredients and stir just until blended. Add the blueberries, almonds, and orange zest, and stir just until combined; do not overmix.

4. Divide the batter evenly among the prepared muffin tin cups and sprinkle the batter lightly with the remaining 1 tablespoon sugar.

5. Bake for 18 to 20 minutes, or until the muffins are golden and cracked on top, and a toothpick inserted in the center of a muffin comes out clean and dry. Serve the muffins warm, or at room temperature.

Makes 1 dozen

Date Nut Bread

For a proper afternoon tea, serve dainty sandwiches of date nut bread spread with cream cheese. Just be sure to let the bread cool completely so that it will be easier to cut into thin slices. If possible, cool it, then wrap it and let it "rest" overnight before slicing. The batter contains pear nectar, which ensures an unusually moist texture.

2 cups flour

1 tablespoon baking powder

1 teaspoon baking soda

¼ teaspoon salt

4 tablespoons butter, softened to room
    temperature

⅓ cup (packed) dark brown sugar

1 egg

1 teaspoon vanilla extract

1 cup pear nectar *— or peach*

1 cup chopped dates

1 cup coarsely chopped pecans

1 tablespoon grated orange zest

excellent

use light brown

1. Preheat the oven to 375°. Butter and flour a 9 x 5-inch loaf pan.

2. In a small bowl, stir together the flour, baking powder, baking soda, and salt.

3. In a large bowl, cream the butter and sugar. Beat in the egg and vanilla. Add half of the dry ingredients, then, alternating between the two, add the pear nectar and the remaining dry ingredients, beating well after each addition. Stir in the dates, pecans, and orange zest.

4. Spread the batter evenly in the prepared pan. Rap the pan once or twice on the counter to remove any air pockets. Bake for 50 to 55 minutes, or until the bread is golden and shrinks from the sides of the pan, and a toothpick inserted in the center of the loaf comes out clean and dry.

5. Let the loaf cool in the pan on a rack, then turn it out to cool completely before slicing.

Makes one 9-inch loaf

Apple Cinnamon Muffins

Fresh tart apples, cinnamon, and cloves give these muffins the heart-warming taste of apple pie. Although pure maple syrup, used as the sweetener here, is expensive, blended pancake syrups, which contain little or no maple sugar, should not be substituted. "Fancy" or "Grade A" maple syrups are readily available, but the stronger flavor of "Grade B" syrup—if you can find it—will come through better in baking.

1 medium Granny Smith apple
   (about 6 ounces)
2 cups flour
1 tablespoon baking powder
½ teaspoon baking soda
1 teaspoon cinnamon
¼ teaspoon ground cloves

¼ teaspoon salt
2 eggs, lightly beaten
1 cup plain yogurt
¼ cup maple syrup
3 tablespoons butter, melted
¾ cup coarsely chopped walnuts
2 tablespoons sugar

1. Preheat the oven to 425°. Butter and flour 12 muffin tin cups, or line them with paper baking cups.

2. Core and finely chop the unpeeled apple; set aside.

3. In a large bowl, stir together the flour, baking powder, baking soda, ½ teaspoon of the cinnamon, the cloves, and salt, and make a well in the center.

4. In a small bowl, stir together the eggs, yogurt, maple syrup, and butter. Pour the egg mixture into the dry ingredients and stir just until blended. Add the chopped apple and ½ cup of the walnuts, and stir just until combined; do not overmix.

5. Divide the batter evenly among the prepared muffin tin cups.

6. In a small bowl, combine the sugar with the remaining ½ teaspoon cinnamon and ¼ cup walnuts, and sprinkle the batter with this mixture. Bake for 13 to 18 minutes, or until the tops of the muffins are golden and a toothpick inserted in the center of a muffin comes out clean and dry. Serve warm.

Makes 1 dozen

COOKING WITH GAS

The expression "cooking with gas" has come to mean working quickly and efficiently, and with good reason: for the home baker, the gas stove was a revolution and a revelation. Its oven was fast-heating and easily controllable, while the piped-in fuel meant the end of wood chopping and coal toting.

Although the first gas cooking device was patented in 1805 (the first city gas company was established about ten years later), the fuel was still expensive, and many feared that the gas would flavor the food as it cooked. By the 1880s, however, gas ranges were being produced in volume and sold at popular prices.

The advantages of the gas range for baking were articulated by Betty Lyles Wilson, "America's Foremost Cake Maker," in a circa 1914 stove catalogue: "Your cake will acquire a beautiful golden brown surface and at the same time remain tender and soft. I hold this to be the particular advantage of the Acorn Range."

The biggest technological advance in gas cooking, though, came in 1915, with the introduction of the oven thermostat. The cook no longer had to gauge oven temperature with her hand, or by timing the browning of a sheet of paper. One historian wrote that for the housewife, the oven regulator "marked the real difference between the 19th and 20th centuries." A 1923 brochure for the Lorain Red Wheel heat regulator guaranteed "no anxious moments to the woman using a heat-regulated oven" and proclaimed that "cake put into an oven equipped with a heat regulator requires no watching. One can be assured that . . . it will be properly baked throughout." Another company vowed that temperature control would totally eliminate "the item of luck in baking."

In 1935, the American Gas Association boasted that "Gas cooks foods faster, better, cheaper" with the "instant heat, higher speed and exact shading of temperature only gas can give." By this time, bright enamel had replaced the black iron of the old kitchen range, and the stove had begun to evolve toward its current sleek design. In the early 1940s, as women joined the wartime job force, gas range ads promised "new freedom for women" with self-timers that could turn the oven on and off automatically. An ad from the postwar era conjured up an all-new dream kitchen equipped with a corner "baking center" and a state-of-the-art gas range. By the mid-1950s, some 30 million American households were "cooking with gas," and the energy-efficient gas range remains popular with home bakers to this day.

Green Tomato and Apple Bread

Many gardeners end up with lots of green tomatoes in the fall, when they must be picked hurriedly to save them from frost. Stored in a cool place, covered with sheets of newspaper, green tomatoes will slowly ripen. Meanwhile, there will be a stock of green tomatoes for baking (and for frying and preserving). In this recipe, a second large apple can be substituted for the green tomato, if necessary.

3 cups flour
½ cup (packed) light brown sugar
2 teaspoons baking powder
¾ teaspoon baking soda
½ teaspoon salt
1 teaspoon cinnamon
½ teaspoon ground ginger
¼ teaspoon nutmeg

2 eggs
1 stick (4 ounces) butter, melted
½ cup buttermilk, or ½ cup milk plus
   1½ teaspoons vinegar
1 medium apple, such as Granny Smith,
   unpeeled, coarsely chopped
1 medium green tomato, coarsely chopped
1 cup coarsely chopped pecans

1. Preheat the oven to 350°. Butter and flour a 9 x 5-inch loaf pan.
2. In a medium bowl, stir together the flour, sugar, baking powder, baking soda, salt, cinnamon, ginger, and nutmeg.
3. In a large bowl, beat the eggs until light and fluffy. Beat in the butter and buttermilk. Gradually add the dry ingredients, beating well after each addition. Add the chopped apple, tomato, and pecans, and stir just until combined.
4. Spread the batter evenly in the prepared pan. Rap the pan once or twice on the counter to remove any air pockets. Bake for 1 hour and 10 minutes to 1 hour and 20 minutes, or until the bread is golden-brown and shrinks from the sides of the pan, and a toothpick inserted in the center of the loaf comes out clean and dry.
5. Let the loaf cool in the pan on a rack, then turn it out to cool completely before slicing.

Makes one 9-inch loaf

Cranberry Muffins

The cranberry, which is native to North America, grows wild from Newfoundland to North Carolina. However, almost all of today's commercially cultivated berries come from Massachusetts, Wisconsin, New Jersey, Washington, and Oregon.

1½ cups cranberries
1¾ cups flour
⅔ cup plus 2 tablespoons sugar
½ cup yellow cornmeal
1 tablespoon baking powder
½ teaspoon baking soda

¼ teaspoon salt
2 eggs, lightly beaten
¾ cup buttermilk, or ¾ cup milk plus
   2¼ teaspoons vinegar
4 tablespoons butter, melted
1 teaspoon vanilla extract

*N*ext time you unwrap a stick of butter for baking, consider the complexities of buttermaking as delineated in an 18th-century cookbook: First the cows had to be "milk'd at regular and stated hours." Then, for the cream to rise properly, "the heat of the milk and its depth in the vessel" had to be carefully regulated. Finally, the milk needed to be churned at just the right speed: butter churned too quickly will be "soft and frothy"; while butter churned too slowly "loses its flavor and texture."

Cranberry Muffins

1. Preheat the oven to 400°. Butter and flour 6 large (3½-inch) muffin tin cups (or 16 regular-size cups), or line them with paper baking cups.

2. In a food processor or by hand, coarsely chop the cranberries.

3. In a large bowl, stir together the flour, ⅔ cup of the sugar, the cornmeal, baking powder, baking soda, and salt, and make a well in the center.

4. In a small bowl, stir together the eggs, buttermilk, butter, and vanilla. Pour the egg mixture into the dry ingredients and stir just until blended. Add the chopped cranberries and stir just until combined; do not overmix.

5. Divide the batter evenly among the prepared muffin tin cups and sprinkle the tops of the muffins with the remaining 2 tablespoons sugar. Bake for 20 to 25 minutes (check regular-size muffins after 18 minutes), or until the muffins are golden and cracked on top, and a toothpick inserted in the center of a muffin comes out clean and dry. Serve warm. *Makes 6 large or 16 regular-size muffins*

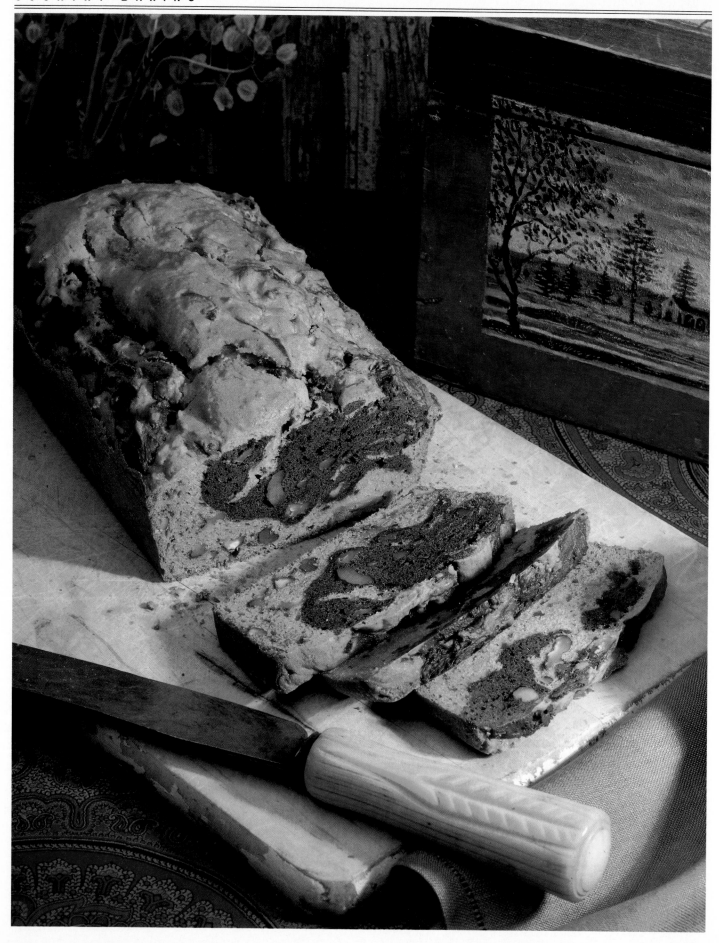

Sweet Potato Swirl Bread

This colorful bread is laced with dark swirls of cocoa, a pleasant counterpoint to the sweetness of the potatoes. Whenever you have leftover sweet potatoes—perhaps after a big holiday meal—this is a delicious and novel way to use them. In cooking potatoes specifically for this recipe, you have several options. Slow baking is the method that brings out their flavor best; it seems to caramelize their natural sugar. However, if you're pressed for time, either cut the sweet potatoes into large chunks and steam them, or pierce the whole potatoes a few times with a fork and microwave them at 100% (high) power for 5 to 8 minutes.

1¾ cups flour

1 teaspoon baking soda

Pinch of salt

1 stick (4 ounces) butter, softened to room temperature

1 cup (packed) light brown sugar

2 eggs

1 teaspoon vanilla extract

1½ cups cooked, peeled, and mashed sweet potatoes (about 2 medium, 2¾ pounds total)

1 cup coarsely chopped walnuts

⅓ cup unsweetened cocoa powder

1. Preheat the oven to 350°. Butter and flour a 9 x 5-inch loaf pan.

2. In a small bowl, stir together the flour, baking soda, and salt; set aside.

3. In a medium bowl, cream the butter and sugar. Beat in the eggs one at a time, beating well after each addition, then beat in the vanilla. Stir in the sweet potatoes until thoroughly combined, then gradually add the dry ingredients, beating just until incorporated; do not overbeat. Stir in the walnuts.

4. Transfer one-third of the batter (about 1½ cups) to a small bowl, add the cocoa powder, and stir until well blended.

5. Spread the plain batter in the prepared pan, then spread the cocoa batter on top. Swirl a table knife through the batter to marbleize it. Rap the pan once or twice on the counter to remove any air pockets.

6. Bake for 1 hour to 1 hour and 10 minutes, or until the bread shrinks from the sides of the pan and a toothpick inserted in the center of the loaf comes out clean and dry.

7. Let the loaf cool in the pan on a rack, then turn it out to cool completely before slicing.

Makes one 9-inch loaf

The Carolina Housewife by a Lady of Charleston was published in 1847. Sarah Rutledge, who compiled the book, apparently knew her potatoes, both white and sweet. "Among the various ways of dressing sweet potatoes," she wrote, "that which appears the most generally preferred, is to bake them twice . . . . This way of baking twice, makes them more candied."

Sweet Potato Swirl Bread

Apricot-Cheese Coffee Ring

Some fortunate American bakers have inherited recipes for fruit-filled European breads—German kuchen, Austrian kugelhopf, Russian kulich, or Czechoslovakian kolacky. Here is a fine all-American version to add to such a collection, or a good starting point for one.

PASTRY
¼ cup lukewarm (105° to 115°)
   water
1 package active dry yeast
2 tablespoons sugar
¼ cup buttermilk or milk
⅓ cup milk
1 egg, lightly beaten
½ teaspoon vanilla extract
About 3½ cups flour
¼ teaspoon salt
⅓ cup chopped blanched almonds
4 tablespoons butter, softened to room
   temperature

FILLING
1 package (3 ounces) cream cheese
¼ cup cottage cheese
1 tablespoon flour
2 tablespoons sugar
1 egg yolk
1 teaspoon lemon juice
1 teaspoon grated lemon zest
16 dried apricot halves
¼ cup apricot preserves

GLAZE
1 egg yolk
1 tablespoon milk

1. Make the pastry: Place the water in a small bowl and sprinkle the yeast over it. Stir in a pinch of sugar and let the mixture stand until the yeast begins to foam, about 5 minutes.

2. Meanwhile, in a small bowl, stir together the remaining sugar, the buttermilk, milk, egg, and vanilla; set aside.

3. In a large bowl, stir together 2½ cups of flour and the salt, and make a well in the center. Pour in the yeast mixture, the milk mixture, and the almonds, and stir until the mixture forms a soft dough. Add the butter and mix until well combined.

4. Transfer the dough to a lightly floured surface and knead it until smooth and elastic, about 10 minutes, adding up to 1 cup more flour if necessary. Form the dough into a ball and place it in a large greased bowl. Cover the bowl with a slightly dampened kitchen towel, set it aside in a warm, draft-free place, and let the dough rise until it doubles in bulk, 45 minutes to 1 hour.

5. Meanwhile, make the filling: In a food processor or blender, combine the cream cheese, cottage cheese, and flour, and process until smooth. Add the sugar, egg yolk, lemon juice and zest, and process just until blended; set aside.

6. Grease and flour two baking sheets.

7. Punch the dough down, then transfer it to a lightly floured surface and knead it for 2 to 3 minutes. Divide the dough into 2 portions.

8. Roll one portion of dough into an 18-inch rope and place it on a prepared baking sheet (see Shaped Pastries, pages 132-133, for step-by-step photos). Bring the ends of the rope together to form a ring; overlap and pinch the ends together. Flatten the ring of dough to a width of about 3 inches. Using a sharp knife, make eight dia-

gonal cuts about 2 inches apart through the outside edge of the ring. The cuts should come to within about 1 inch of the inside edge.

9. Spread half the cream cheese mixture around the inner (uncut) portion of the ring, then arrange 8 apricots on top. Top the apricots with half the preserves.

10. Fold the long points of the flaps of dough around the apricot halves and tack them down with a few drops of egg yolk. Press a bit of dough from the center of the ring over each point to seal it; reserve the remaining egg yolk.

11. Shape the second portion of dough in the same fashion, then set both rings aside, uncovered, in a warm, draft-free place and let rise for 20 to 25 minutes, or until doubled in bulk.

12. Preheat the oven to 375°. For the glaze, stir the milk into the reserved egg yolk. Brush one ring with half of the glaze and bake for 15 to 20 minutes, or until golden brown. (Leave the second ring in the refrigerator until ready to bake, but no longer than 1 hour.)

13. Transfer the baked apricot ring to a rack to cool. Meanwhile, glaze and bake the second ring.

Makes two 10-inch rings

Strawberries and Cream Bread

M.T. Colbrath's *What to Get for Breakfast*, published in 1890, offered more than a hundred menus for that meal. Two included strawberry shortcake—in fact, a chapter was devoted to "dainty and delicious fruit-cake breakfasts for those who cannot relish hearty food for a summer breakfast." Here, shortcake's basic ingredients—including berries and cream—are transformed into a luscious, fragrant bread.

2 cups flour	2 eggs
½ cup sugar	¼ cup heavy cream
1 tablespoon baking powder	4 tablespoons butter, melted
½ teaspoon baking soda	1 teaspoon vanilla extract
½ teaspoon salt	1¼ cups strawberries, mashed (about 1 cup)

1. Preheat the oven to 350°. Butter and flour a 9 x 5-inch loaf pan.

2. In a large bowl, stir together the flour, sugar, baking powder, baking soda, and salt.

3. In a small bowl, stir together the eggs, cream, butter, and vanilla. Pour the egg mixture into the dry ingredients and mix just until blended. Add the strawberries, and stir just until combined; do not overmix.

4. Spread the batter evenly in the prepared pan. Rap the pan once or twice on the counter to remove any air pockets. Bake for 1 hour to 1 hour and 10 minutes, or until the bread is golden and shrinks from the sides of the pan, and a toothpick inserted in the center of the loaf comes out clean and dry.

5. Let the loaf cool in the pan on a rack, then turn it out to cool completely before slicing.

Makes one 9-inch loaf

SHAPED PASTRIES

JAM PINWHEELS

Here are step-by-step photographs for forming Jam Pinwheels (recipe on page 137). Complete Steps 1-5 of the recipe, then proceed with the technique shown at right. This recipe makes twenty 3-inch-square pastries; an average-sized baking sheet will hold about half of them. If you have two baking sheets, prepare both batches at once, but keep one refrigerated (for no longer than one hour) while you bake the other.

Roll out the dough to a rectangle roughly 15 x 12 inches. Use a ruler to trim the dough to the exact measurement, then cut it into twenty 3-inch squares.

Place the squares on a greased baking sheet. With a sharp knife, make diagonal cuts from the corners of each square to within ¾ inch of the center.

APRICOT-CHEESE COFFEE RING

Here are step-by-step photographs for forming the Apricot-Cheese Coffee Ring (recipe on page 130). Complete Steps 1-7 of the recipe, then proceed with the technique at right. The recipe makes two 10-inch coffee rings, which will have to be baked separately. Assemble both rings and let them rise at the same time, but refrigerate one of the rings (for no longer than 1 hour) while you bake the other.

Roll one portion of the dough into an 18-inch rope. On a greased baking sheet, form the dough into a ring and flatten to a width of about 3 inches.

Using a knife or scissors, make diagonal cuts, about 2 inches apart, around the outside edge of the ring. The cuts should come to within 1 inch of the inside edge.

APPLE-FILLED CRISSCROSS

Here are step-by-step photographs for forming the Apple-Filled Crisscross (recipe on page 134). Complete Steps 1-8 of the recipe, then proceed with the technique at right. Although a large baking sheet will hold the two loaves, they can also be baked separately. Assemble both loaves and let them rise at the same time, but refrigerate one of the loaves (for no longer than 1 hour) while you bake the other.

Spread half the apple filling in a 2-inch-wide strip down the center of one rectangle of dough, leaving a border of about ½ inch at both of the short ends.

With a sharp knife, make an equal number of diagonal cuts along both long sides of the rectangle of dough, ½ inch apart and to within ½ inch of the apple filling.

Place ½ teaspoon of jam in the center of each square. For variety, use different jam flavors and colors. Do not substitute jelly, which will melt in the heat of the oven.

Fold every other point of the cut pastry in to the right of center and tack it in place with beaten egg yolk. The points should not completely cover the jam.

Let the pastries rise until almost doubled. Brush with egg glaze and bake in a 375° oven for 15 to 20 minutes, or until golden brown. Repeat with second batch.

Spread half the cream cheese mixture on the uncut portion of the ring, then arrange eight dried apricots on top. Top the apricots with half of the preserves.

Fold the points of cut dough in toward the center of the ring, partially covering the apricots. Tack the points of dough in place with some beaten egg yolk.

Let the ring rise until doubled, then brush with egg glaze and bake in a 375° oven for 15 to 20 minutes, or until golden brown. Repeat with the second ring.

Bring the strips of dough up and over the filling in crisscross fashion. Overlap the ends of the strips slightly and pinch them together to seal.

Tuck the end pieces under and pinch together to form a small retaining wall for the filling at both ends. Set the loaf aside to rise until almost doubled.

Brush the loaf with egg glaze and then bake in a 375° oven for about 15 minutes, or until golden brown. Repeat with the second loaf.

133

Apple-Filled Crisscross

The filling of these latticed loaves is reminiscent of apple strudel, but the rich sour-cream dough is much easier to work with than fragile, paper-thin strudel dough. For ease in shaping the loaves, the strips of dough are simply crisscrossed, not braided, over the chunky apple-raisin-walnut filling.

Northern Spy, Newtown Pippin, Sweet Bough, Black Twig, Jonathan, Twenty Ounce, Wealthy, Winesap, Roxbury Russet, Grimes Golden—the names of America's old apple varieties form a sweet poetry all their own. More and more growers around the country are devoting their efforts to preserving "antique" fruit varieties. Look for old-fashioned apples at farm markets and orchard stands; sample their varied flavors and textures, and ask about their best uses.

PASTRY
¼ cup lukewarm (105° to 115°) water
1 package active dry yeast
¼ cup granulated sugar
⅓ cup sour cream, at room temperature
2 tablespoons lukewarm (105 to 115°) milk
1 egg, lightly beaten
1 teaspoon grated lemon zest
½ teaspoon vanilla extract
About 3 cups flour
¼ teaspoon salt
6 tablespoons butter, softened to room temperature

FILLING
1 small apple, such as Granny Smith or Golden Delicious, unpeeled and coarsely chopped

¼ cup raisins
3 tablespoons coarse fresh breadcrumbs
¼ cup coarsely chopped walnuts
2 tablespoons sugar
½ teaspoon cinnamon
¼ teaspoon grated lemon zest
1 teaspoon lemon juice

EGG GLAZE
1 egg yolk
1 tablespoon milk

ICING
1 cup confectioners' sugar
2 tablespoons lemon juice

1. Make the pastry: Place the water in a small bowl and sprinkle the yeast over it. Stir in a large pinch of granulated sugar and let the mixture stand until the yeast begins to foam, about 5 minutes.

2. In a small bowl, stir together the remaining granulated sugar, the sour cream, milk, egg, lemon zest, and vanilla; set aside.

3. In a large bowl, stir together 2½ cups of flour and the salt, and make a well in the center. Pour in the yeast mixture and the milk mixture, and stir until the mixture forms a soft dough.

4. Add the butter and mix until well combined. Transfer the dough to a lightly floured surface and knead it until smooth and elastic, about 10 minutes, adding up to ½ cup more flour if necessary. Form the dough into a ball and place it in a large greased bowl. Cover the bowl with a slightly dampened kitchen towel, set it aside in a warm, draft-free place, and let the dough rise until it doubles in bulk, 45 minutes to 1 hour.

5. Meanwhile, make the filling: In a medium bowl, stir together the chopped apple, raisins, breadcrumbs, nuts, granulated sugar, cinnamon, lemon zest, and lemon juice; set aside.

6. Grease and flour two baking sheets.

7. Punch the dough down, then transfer it to a lightly floured surface and knead it for about 5 minutes.

Apple-Filled Crisscross

8. Using a lightly floured rolling pin, roll out the dough to an 18 x 8-inch rectangle, then cut it into two 9 x 8-inch rectangles. Place each rectangle of dough on a prepared baking sheet.

9. Spread half of the apple filling in a 2-inch-wide strip down the center of each piece of dough, leaving a border of about ½ inch at the top and bottom (see Shaped Pastries, pages 132-133, for step-by-step photos). Starting ½ inch from the filling, make diagonal cuts ½ inch apart, from the filling out to the edges of the dough, on both sides. Crisscross the strips over the filling. Tuck the last two strips under and press firmly to seal them.

10. Set the loaves aside, uncovered, in a warm, draft-free place and let the dough rise for 20 to 25 minutes, or until almost doubled in bulk.

11. Preheat the oven to 375°.

12. Make the egg glaze: In a small bowl, stir together the egg yolk and milk.

13. Brush one loaf with half of the egg glaze and bake for 15 to 17 minutes, or until golden brown. (Leave the second loaf in the refrigerator until ready to bake, but no longer than 1 hour.)

14. Transfer the baked loaf to a rack to cool. Meanwhile, glaze and bake the second loaf.

15. Make the icing: In a medium bowl, stir together the confectioners' sugar and lemon juice until smooth and pourable; add a few drops more lemon juice, if necessary. Drizzle the icing over both loaves while still warm.

Makes two 9-inch loaves

Jam Pinwheels

An appealing offering at a festive breakfast, these pinwheels are a less-rich version of what Americans know as Danish pastry. In Denmark, such pastries—served for breakfast, snacks, and dessert—are called *Wienerbrød*, meaning Viennese bread, because the recipes and techniques were brought to Denmark by Austrians.

¾ cup plus 1 tablespoon milk

1 package active dry yeast

1 egg, lightly beaten, plus 1 egg yolk

4 tablespoons butter, melted

⅓ cup sugar

About 2½ cups flour

¼ teaspoon salt

About ¼ cup jam

1. In a small saucepan, heat ¼ cup of the milk over medium heat to almost boiling. Remove the pan from the heat and let the milk cool to lukewarm (105° to 115°). Sprinkle the yeast over the milk and stir until dissolved; set aside.

2. In a small bowl, stir together ½ cup of the remaining milk, the whole egg, butter, and sugar.

3. In a large bowl, stir together 2 cups of the flour and the salt, and make a well in the center. Pour in the yeast mixture and the milk mixture, and stir until a soft dough is formed.

4. Transfer the dough to a lightly floured surface and knead it until smooth and elastic, about 10 minutes, adding up to ½ cup more flour if necessary. Form the dough into a ball and place it in a large greased bowl. Cover the bowl with a slightly dampened kitchen towel, set it aside in a warm, draft-free place, and let the dough rise until it doubles in bulk, 45 minutes to 1 hour.

5. Lightly grease a baking sheet. Punch the dough down, then transfer it to a lightly floured surface and knead it for about 2 minutes.

6. Using a lightly floured rolling pin, roll out the dough to a rectangle roughly 15 x 12 inches. Use a ruler to trim the dough to the exact measurement (see Shaped Pastries, pages 132-133, for step-by-step photos). Using a sharp knife, cut the dough into twenty 3-inch squares.

7. Transfer the squares of dough to the prepared baking sheet. Make diagonal cuts from the corners of each square to within about ¾ inch of the center.

8. In a small bowl, beat the remaining egg yolk.

9. Place ½ teaspoon of jam in the center of each square. Fold every other point toward the center (the dough should not completely cover the jam) to form pinwheels, and seal the points with a drop of egg yolk. Tuck the last point under the pastry.

10. Set the pastries aside, uncovered, in a warm, draft-free place to rise for 20 to 25 minutes; the dough should not double in bulk.

11. Preheat the oven to 375°. Meanwhile, make an egg glaze by beating the remaining egg yolk with the remaining 1 tablespoon milk.

12. Brush the pastries with the glaze and bake for 15 to 20 minutes, or until golden brown and firm. Let the pastries cool on the baking sheet for 2 to 3 minutes, then transfer them to a rack to cool further. *Makes 20 pinwheels*

Jam Pinwheels

137

Chili-Cheese Corn Muffins

These savory muffins are an excellent accompaniment to eggs. Serve them with *huevos rancheros*, or make a South-of-the-Border version of eggs Benedict by splitting the muffins, then topping them with ham, poached eggs, and a spicy cheese sauce. For fans of hot chilies, substitute jalapeños for the mild green chilies.

1 cup yellow cornmeal
1 cup flour
1 tablespoon baking powder
½ teaspoon baking soda
½ teaspoon salt
½ teaspoon chili powder
2 eggs, lightly beaten

¼ cup sour cream
3 tablespoons butter, melted
1 can (8 ounces) cream-style corn
1 cup grated yellow Cheddar cheese
  (about ¼ pound)
1 can (4 ounces) chopped mild green
  chilies, drained

1. Preheat the oven to 425°. Butter and flour 12 muffin tin cups, or line them with paper baking cups.

2. In a large bowl, stir together the cornmeal, flour, baking powder, baking soda, salt, and chili powder, and make a well in the center.

3. In a small bowl, stir together the eggs, sour cream, and butter. Pour the egg mixture into the dry ingredients and mix just until blended. Add the corn, Cheddar cheese, and chilies, and stir just until combined; do not overmix.

4. Divide the batter evenly among the prepared muffin tin cups and bake for 15 to 18 minutes, or until the tops of the muffins are golden and a toothpick inserted in the center of a muffin comes out clean and dry. Serve the muffins warm. *Makes 1 dozen*

Soda Bread with Golden Raisins

Ireland's traditional bread is especially popular around St. Patrick's Day, but it is so tasty that there's no reason to bake it only for that holiday. Soda bread is easy to make, requiring no rising time and only a moment's kneading. This version contains whole-wheat flour for an unusually hearty flavor. The bread is delicious fresh or toasted, spread generously with butter.

About 2¾ cups all-purpose flour
¾ cup whole-wheat flour
1 teaspoon baking powder
1 teaspoon baking soda
1 teaspoon salt

1 tablespoon caraway seeds
1½ cups buttermilk
3 tablespoons honey
4 tablespoons chilled butter, cut into pieces
1 cup golden raisins

1. Preheat the oven to 375°. Lightly grease and flour a baking sheet.

2. In a large bowl, stir together 2½ cups of the all-purpose flour, the whole-wheat flour, baking powder, baking soda, salt, and caraway seeds; set aside.

3. In a small bowl, stir together the buttermilk and honey; set aside.

4. Using a pastry blender or two knives, cut the butter into the dry ingredients until the mixture resembles coarse crumbs. Stir in the raisins, then make a well in the center. Pour in the buttermilk mixture and stir until blended; the dough will be sticky.

5. Place the dough on a generously floured surface and knead it for 1 minute, adding up to ¼ cup more all-purpose flour if necessary to keep the dough from sticking. Shape the dough into a round loaf and place it on the prepared baking sheet. Using a floured sharp knife or razor blade, cut an X about ¼ inch deep in the top of the dough.

6. Bake for 45 to 50 minutes, or until the bread is golden and a toothpick inserted in the center of the loaf comes out clean and dry.

7. Turn the loaf out onto a rack to cool before slicing. *Makes one 9-inch loaf*

Zucchini-Pecan Bread

These mildly sweet loaves are another example of the thrifty—and imaginative—American cooking spirit at work. What gardener hasn't wondered what to do with an overabundant harvest of zucchini? This recipe solves the problem beautifully.

1½ cups flour
1 teaspoon baking powder
½ teaspoon baking soda
½ teaspoon salt
2 eggs
½ cup vegetable oil

¾ cup sugar
1 cup grated zucchini (about ¼ pound
  fresh zucchini)
1 teaspoon vanilla extract
1 cup coarsely chopped pecans

1. Preheat the oven to 350°. Butter and flour two 5¾ x 3-inch loaf pans (or one 9 x 5-inch loaf pan).

2. In a medium bowl, stir together the flour, baking powder, baking soda, and salt; set aside.

3. In a large bowl, beat together the eggs and oil. Beat in the sugar, grated zucchini, and vanilla extract. Gradually add the dry ingredients, stirring just until incorporated. Stir in the pecans.

4. Spread the batter evenly in the prepared pans. Rap the pans once or twice on the counter to remove any air pockets. Bake for 45 to 50 minutes, or until the bread is golden brown and shrinks from the sides of the pan, and a toothpick inserted in the center of the loaf comes out clean and dry.

5. Let the loaves cool in the pans on a rack, then turn them out to cool completely before slicing. *Makes 2 small loaves or 1 large loaf*

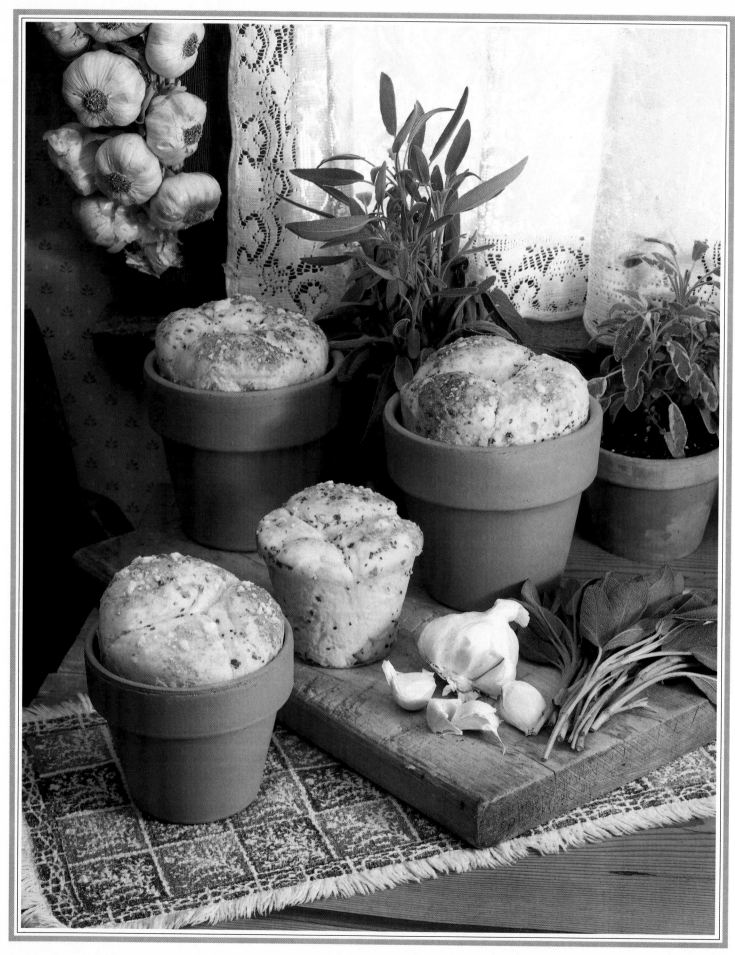

Breads, Biscuits, and Crackers

country baking with wholesome grains

Making bread twice weekly—or even daily—is no longer the unavoidable chore it once was; bread baking is now done by choice, for the pure pleasure of it. Today bread bakers can be justifiably proud of their skills, for turning out handsomely risen, golden loaves is almost a lost art.

Although bread making does take practice, the basic steps are easy to master, and the outcome is almost always rewarding. If you've never baked bread before, start with a basic recipe such as five-grain loaf, and work up to more ambitious endeavors, such as forming cloverleaf dinner rolls. The biscuit and cracker recipes in this chapter are also simple to follow; let them help you perfect your baking skills, lest, in the words of an 1872 cookbook author, you find yourself "among those who are ashamed to know how to make a loaf of bread or to stir a batch of biscuit with their own hands."

Savory Garlic-Sage Flowerpot Breads are charming "conversation starters."

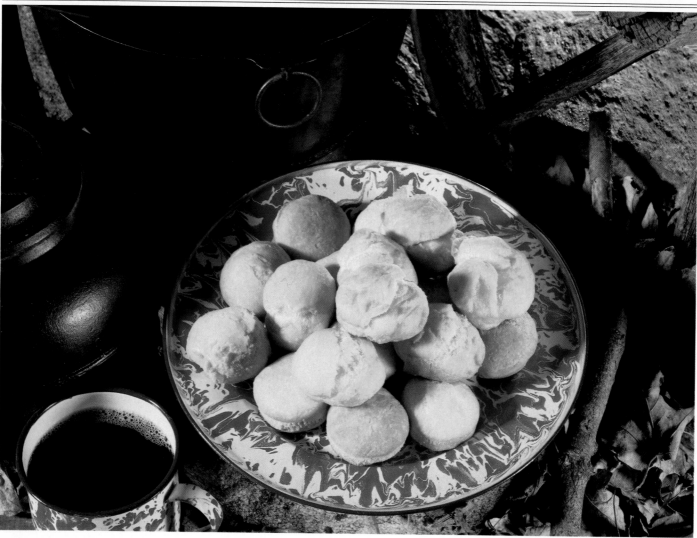

Cowboy Biscuits

Cowboy Biscuits

Part of a Southwestern tradition of fried breads that includes New Mexican *sopai-pillas* and Navajo fry-bread, these puffy, golden biscuits are crisp on the outside and soft on the inside. They cook in minutes and should be served piping hot.

2 cups flour

1 teaspoon baking soda

½ teaspoon salt

¼ teaspoon baking powder

¼ teaspoon cream of tartar

4 tablespoons chilled butter, cut into pieces

About 1 cup buttermilk, or 1 cup milk plus
   1 tablespoon vinegar

3-pound can vegetable shortening, or
   7 cups vegetable oil

1. In a medium bowl, stir together the flour, baking soda, salt, baking powder, and cream of tartar. Using a pastry blender or two knives, cut in the butter until the mixture resembles coarse meal. Stir in just enough buttermilk (¾ to 1 cup) to make a smooth dough. Form the dough into a ball.

2. Transfer the dough to a lightly floured surface and knead it briefly. Using a floured rolling pin, roll out the dough to a ½-inch thickness. With a floured 2¼-inch round biscuit cutter, cut out 12 biscuits. Gather, reroll, and cut any scraps.

3. In a Dutch oven or large, heavy flameproof casserole, heat the vegetable shortening over medium heat until very hot but not smoking (375°). Carefully place the biscuits, two at a time, in the hot oil, turning them with a slotted spoon to coat them on all sides. When all the biscuits are in the pot, fry them for 4 minutes.

4. Turn the biscuits over and fry until they are evenly browned and puffed, about 4 minutes longer. Using a slotted spoon, transfer the biscuits to paper towels to drain for a moment. Serve hot.

Makes about 1 dozen

Corn Crackers

If you've never made crackers before, you may be surprised at the simplicity of the technique. These light corn crackers, with their mildly spicy taste and crunchy texture, provide the perfect accompaniment to such Tex-Mex party fare as salsa and guacamole. Double the recipe if you are serving a crowd.

1 cup yellow cornmeal	*½ teaspoon baking soda*
⅓ cup flour	*¼ teaspoon pepper*
1½ teaspoons chili powder	*⅓ cup plain yogurt*
1 teaspoon sugar	*3 tablespoons chopped fresh coriander*
1 teaspoon ground cumin	*2 tablespoons corn oil*
¾ teaspoon salt	*1 to 2 tablespoons milk*

1. Preheat the oven to 350°. Lightly grease a baking sheet.

2. In a medium bowl, stir together the cornmeal, flour, chili powder, sugar, cumin, salt, baking soda, and pepper.

3. In a small bowl, stir together the yogurt, coriander, corn oil, and 1 tablespoon of milk. Add the yogurt mixture to the dry ingredients and stir until a soft dough forms, adding up to 1 tablespoon more milk, if necessary.

4. Divide the dough in half. Place one portion of dough on the prepared baking sheet and pat it into a square shape. Using a rolling pin lightly dusted with cornmeal, roll out the dough to a square roughly 5 x 5 inches. Place a sheet of plastic wrap over the dough and continue rolling it out to roughly 10 x 10 inches; remove the plastic wrap and use a ruler to trim the dough to the exact measurement.

5. Cut the dough into 2-inch squares, then cut each square diagonally into triangles. (Cut all the way through the dough, but do not separate the crackers.) Bake for 20 minutes, or until the crackers are crisp and golden, turning the baking sheet after about 8 minutes.

6. Let the crackers cool on the baking sheet for 1 minute, then separate them and transfer them to a rack to cool completely. Repeat with the second portion of dough.

Makes 100

P ractical Housekeeping, published in 1892, included a recipe for fried biscuits made from risen bread dough: "If the wheat bread is light enough for the oven at breakfast time, have ready some hot lard in a deep kettle; with the thumb and two fingers pull up some of the dough quite thin, and cut it some two or three inches in length; as these pieces are cut, drop them in the lard and fry like doughnuts. At table they are eaten like biscuit. . . "

Cheddar-Chive Swirls

The recipe for these cheese-swirled rolls can also be used to make an impressive ring-shaped loaf: see A Savory Filled Bread on pages 146-147 for step-by-step photos.

¼ cup lukewarm (105° to 115°) water
1 package active dry yeast
1 tablespoon sugar
¾ cup plus 2 tablespoons milk
About 3 cups flour
¾ teaspoon salt
4 tablespoons butter, softened

2 cups grated Cheddar cheese
  (about 8 ounces)
2 cups chopped chives or scallion
  greens
½ teaspoon pepper
1 egg yolk

1. Place the water in a small bowl and sprinkle the yeast over it. Stir in the sugar and let stand until the yeast begins to foam, about 5 minutes.

2. In a small saucepan, heat ¾ cup of the milk to lukewarm (105° to 115°).

3. In a large bowl, stir together 2½ cups of the flour and the salt, and make a well in the center. Pour in the yeast mixture and the warm milk, and stir until the mixture forms a smooth dough. Blend in 2 tablespoons of the butter.

4. Transfer the dough to a lightly floured surface and knead it until smooth and elastic, about 10 minutes, adding up to ½ cup more flour if necessary. Form the dough into a ball and place it in a large greased bowl. Cover the bowl with a slightly dampened kitchen towel, set it aside in a warm, draft-free place, and let the dough rise until it doubles in bulk, 45 minutes to 1 hour.

5. Lightly grease 2 baking sheets.

6. Punch the dough down, then transfer it to a lightly floured surface. Divide the dough in half. Using a lightly floured rolling pin, roll each piece of dough out to a 10 x 9-inch rectangle.

7. Brush the rectangles of dough with the remaining 2 tablespoons butter. Sprinkle half the cheese, chives, and pepper over each piece of dough, leaving a ½-inch border on each side. With the rolling pin, gently press the filling into the dough.

8. Starting at one long side, tightly roll each piece of dough jelly-roll fashion, and pinch the seam to seal it. Cut each roll crosswise into 6 pieces. Place 6 rolls, seam-side down, on each of the prepared baking sheets, leaving 3 inches of space between the rolls. Using kitchen scissors, make two parallel cuts three-quarters of the way into each roll. Gently fan out the sections of each roll to expose the filling. Set aside, uncovered, in a warm, draft-free place and let rise until the dough doubles in bulk, about 25 minutes.

9. Preheat the oven to 375°. In a small bowl, beat the egg yolk with the remaining 2 tablespoons milk to make a glaze.

10. Brush one sheet of rolls with the glaze and bake for 15 to 20 minutes, or until golden brown. (Cover the second sheet of rolls loosely with plastic wrap and leave it in the refrigerator until ready to bake, but no longer than 1 hour.) Transfer the rolls to a rack to cool for at least 10 minutes. Meanwhile, glaze and bake the second sheet of rolls. Serve warm, or at room temperature.

Makes 1 dozen

Cheddar-Chive Swirls

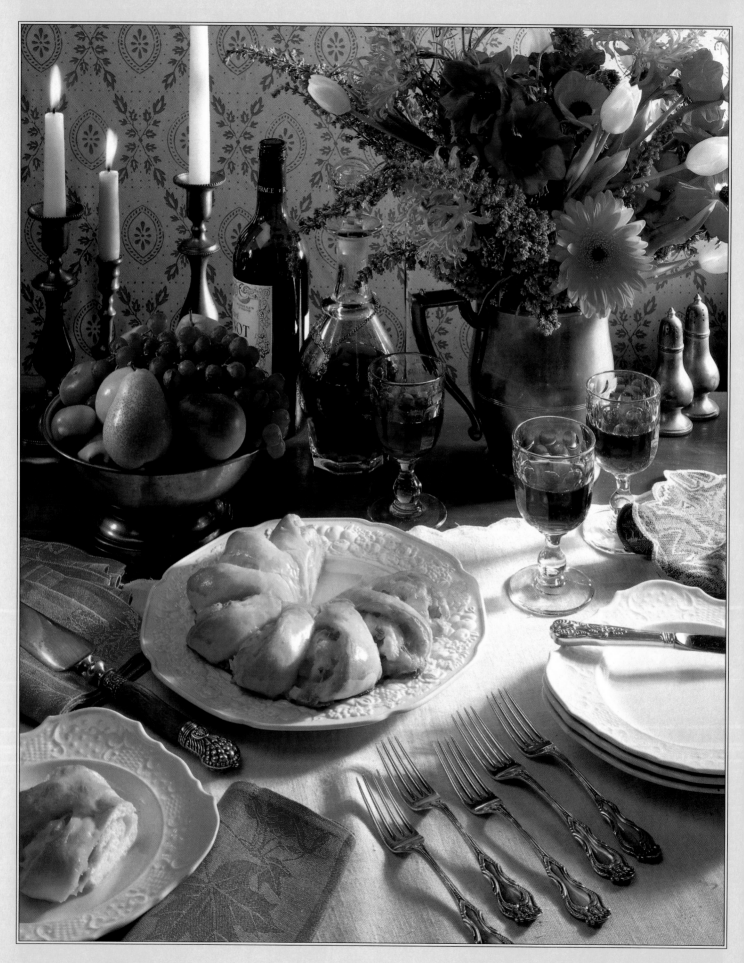

A Savory Filled Bread

Divide the dough into two portions and roll each portion into a 10 x 9-inch rectangle. Brush each rectangle with 1 tablespoon of softened butter.

Sprinkle each rectangle with half the filling, leaving a border of ½ inch all around. Press the filling lightly into the dough with a rolling pin.

Starting at one long side, tightly roll up each rectangle of dough jelly-roll fashion. Pinch the raw edges of dough against the roll to form a smooth seam.

Place the roll, seam side down, on a greased baking sheet and shape it into a ring. Pinch the ends together to seal. Repeat with the second roll.

With a sharp knife, make cuts 1½ inches apart all around both rings. The cuts should only go three-quarters of the way through the rings.

Gently fan the cut sections outward. Refrigerate one ring while the other rises. Brush with egg glaze and bake at 375° for about 25 minutes.

Filled breads are especially satisfying examples of the baker's art. This ring-shaped version, Onion-Cheese Ring, is rewarding for the cook and diners alike. It can be offered by itself as an appetizer, or served with soup or salad as a lunch or a light dinner.

Onion-Cheese Ring is actually a variation on Cheddar-Chive Swirls (page 144), which are individual rolls made with the same basic ingredients and shaped in a similar fashion. To prepare the Onion-Cheese Ring, use the Cheddar-Chive Swirls recipe, but make the following adjustments: Omit the pepper, and substitute 1 cup of finely chopped onion for the chives. (If possible, use red onion, as its pink tones complement the deep yellow of the Cheddar.) Follow the instructions in the Cheddar-Chive Swirls recipe through the first rising (Step 4). Punch the dough down, transfer it to a lightly floured surface, and knead it briefly. Then proceed with the method shown in the step-by-step photographs above.

Though the ring is impressive in appearance, the technique is really quite simple and adaptable. In fact, the same general recipe could be used to make a sweet filled bread to be served for breakfast, or with afternoon tea. Just substitute a sweet filling—such as raisins, chopped dried fruits, chopped nuts, brown sugar, spices, and citrus zest—for the onion-cheese mixture.

Garlic-Sage Flowerpot Breads

Use new terra-cotta pots for baking these breads. Season the pots first by brushing the insides with vegetable oil, then placing them on a baking sheet and heating in a 450° oven for one hour. Cool, wash, and dry the seasoned pots before using them.

10 tablespoons butter

4 cloves garlic, finely chopped

⅓ cup chopped fresh sage, or 1
tablespoon dried

¼ cup lukewarm (105° to 115°) water

1 package active dry yeast

Pinch of sugar

1 cup plain yogurt

1 egg, lightly beaten, plus 1 egg yolk

About 3½ cups flour

¾ teaspoon salt

1 tablespoon milk

1 tablespoon grated Parmesan cheese

1. In a small skillet, melt the butter over medium heat. Add the garlic and sauté until golden, about 5 to 10 minutes. Stir in the sage; set aside.

2. Place the water in a small bowl and sprinkle the yeast over it. Stir in the sugar and let the mixture stand until the yeast begins to foam, about 5 minutes.

3. Meanwhile, in a small bowl, stir together the yogurt and the whole egg. In a large bowl, stir together 3 cups of flour and the salt, and make a well in the center. Pour in the yogurt and yeast mixtures, and stir until the mixture forms a soft dough. Blend in 2 tablespoons of the garlic-sage butter.

4. Transfer the dough to a lightly floured surface and knead it until smooth and elastic, about 10 minutes, adding up to ½ cup more flour if necessary. Form the dough into a ball and place it in a large greased bowl. Cover the bowl with a slightly dampened kitchen towel, set it aside in a warm, draft-free place, and let the dough rise until it doubles in bulk, 45 minutes to 1 hour.

5. Lightly grease 4 small (4 inches across and 3½ inches deep) or 2 medium (4¾ inches across and 4¾ inches deep) flowerpots and line the bottoms with circles of lightly greased parchment or foil.

6. Punch the dough down, then transfer it to a lightly floured surface. Knead the dough for 2 minutes, then divide it into 4 portions. Roll each portion of dough into 5 balls, then dip them in the remaining garlic-sage butter. Place 5 balls of dough in each of the prepared flowerpots (10 balls if using medium pots). Set aside, uncovered, in a warm, draft-free place to rise until doubled in bulk, 30 to 45 minutes.

7. Meanwhile, preheat the oven to 425°. In a small bowl, beat together the remaining egg yolk and the milk to make a glaze.

8. Brush the tops of the loaves with the egg glaze and sprinkle them with the Parmesan. Place the pots on a baking sheet and bake for 15 minutes, then reduce the oven temperature to 375° and bake for another 4 to 6 minutes (up to 8 minutes for medium loaves), or until the tops of the breads are golden brown. Cool the loaves in the pots for 15 minutes, then run the tip of a knife around the edge of each loaf to loosen it and transfer to a rack to cool completely. *Makes 4 small or 2 medium loaves*

Dill Cheese Bread

This rich, eggy bread, made with cottage cheese, has been an American favorite since the 1950s, when it was baked in a deep, round dish and was known as "casserole bread" or "patio bread." This version is made as a simple three-strand braid. If possible, use fresh dill; its flavor is much more intense than that of the dried herb.

¼ cup lukewarm (105° to 115°) water
1 package active dry yeast
2 teaspoons sugar
2 tablespoons butter
½ cup minced scallions
About 3 cups flour
¾ teaspoon salt

¼ teaspoon baking soda
2 eggs
1 cup cottage cheese
¼ cup chopped fresh dill, or 1
*   tablespoon dried*
1 tablespoon milk

1. Place the water in a small bowl and sprinkle the yeast over it. Stir in 1 teaspoon of the sugar and let stand until the yeast begins to foam, about 5 minutes.

2. Meanwhile, in a small skillet, melt the butter over medium heat. Add the scallions and sauté until they are softened but not browned, about 2 minutes; set aside to cool slightly.

3. In a medium bowl, stir together 2½ cups of the flour, the salt, baking soda, and remaining 1 teaspoon sugar, and make a well in the center. In a small bowl, lightly beat one of the eggs.

4. Stir the beaten egg, sautéed scallions, yeast mixture, cottage cheese, and dill into the dry ingredients, and continue stirring until the mixture forms a smooth dough.

5. Transfer the dough to a lightly floured surface and knead it until smooth and elastic, about 10 minutes, adding up to ½ cup more flour if necessary. Form the dough into a ball and place it in a large greased bowl. Set aside, uncovered, in a warm, draft-free place, and let the dough rise until it doubles in bulk, 45 minutes to 1 hour.

6. Lightly grease a baking sheet.

7. Punch the dough down, then transfer it to a lightly floured surface. Divide the dough into 3 portions. Roll each piece of dough into a rope about 15 inches long and 1 inch in diameter. Lay the three ropes side by side on the prepared baking sheet, pinch them together at one end, and braid them. Pinch the other end of the braid together. Cover the braid with a slightly dampened kitchen towel and set aside in a warm, draft-free place to rise until doubled in bulk, 30 to 45 minutes.

8. Preheat the oven to 350°. In a small bowl, beat the remaining egg with the milk to make a glaze.

9. Brush the top of the braid with the glaze and bake for 30 to 35 minutes, or until the bread is golden brown. Cool the bread on the baking sheet for 10 minutes, then transfer it to a rack to cool completely before slicing. *Makes one 18-inch braid*

Cinnamon Raisin Bread

This irresistibly fragrant loaf has walnuts, raisins, and cinnamon mixed into the dough as well as a center swirl filled with cinnamon-sugar and raisins.

1¼ cups milk
¼ cup water
1 package active dry yeast
1 tablespoon granulated sugar
½ cup dark raisins
½ cup golden raisins

About 4 ½ cups flour
½ cup coarsely chopped walnuts
1 tablespoon cinnamon
½ teaspoon salt
4 tablespoons butter, melted
½ cup (packed) dark brown sugar

Mary Henderson, in her 1877 book, Practical Cooking and Dinner Giving, wrote, *"I have remarked before that not one person in a thousand knows how to make good toast. The simplest dishes seem to be the ones oftenest spoiled. If the cook sends to the table a properly made piece of toast, one may judge that she is a scientific cook, and may entertain, at the same time, exalted hopes of her."*

1. In a small saucepan, heat the milk and water until almost boiling. Pour the mixture into a large bowl and let cool to lukewarm (105° to 115°).

2. Sprinkle the yeast over the lukewarm milk mixture. Stir in the granulated sugar and let stand until the yeast begins to foam, about 5 minutes.

3. Place the dark and light raisins in a small bowl and toss to mix them. In a medium bowl, stir together 4 cups of the flour, half of the raisins, the walnuts, 1½ teaspoons of the cinnamon, and the salt.

4. Stir the flour mixture and 3 tablespoons of the butter into the yeast mixture, and beat until well blended.

5. Transfer the dough to a lightly floured surface and knead it for 1 to 2 minutes, adding up to ½ cup more flour if the dough is sticky. Let the dough rest, uncovered, for 10 minutes.

6. Knead the dough until smooth and elastic, about 10 minutes, adding more flour, if necessary, to keep the dough from sticking. Form the dough into a ball and place it in a large greased bowl. Cover the bowl with a slightly dampened kitchen towel, set it aside in a warm, draft-free place, and let the dough rise until it doubles in bulk, about 45 minutes.

7. Lightly grease two 8 x 4½-inch loaf pans. In a small bowl, mix the brown sugar with the remaining 1½ teaspoons cinnamon.

8. Punch the dough down, then transfer it to a lightly floured surface. Using a lightly floured rolling pin, roll out the dough to a 16 x 6-inch rectangle, then cut it into two 8 x 6-inch rectangles. Sprinkle each rectangle of dough with the brown sugar mixture, then with the remaining raisins. Starting at one long side, tightly roll each rectangle of dough jelly-roll fashion and pinch the seam to seal it.

9. Place the loaves, seam-side down, in the prepared pans and press gently to fit them into the corners. Set aside, uncovered, in a warm, draft-free place to rise until the dough is level with the tops of the pans, 30 to 45 minutes.

10. Preheat the oven to 350°.

11. Brush the tops of the loaves with the remaining 1 tablespoon butter and bake for 40 to 45 minutes, or until the tops of the loaves are golden brown. Let the loaves cool in the pans for 10 minutes, then transfer them to a rack to cool completely before slicing.

Makes two 8-inch loaves

Soda Crackers

The cracker barrel, proverbial centerpiece of the country general store, was the soda cracker source for several generations. But before store-bought crackers there were home-baked, which you can duplicate with this recipe. The technique of folding the dough, also used in making puff pastry, gives these crackers an especially flaky texture. The longer the dough rests, the easier it will be to handle. For the best results, mix the dough the day before you plan to bake, and refrigerate it overnight.

¼ cup lukewarm (105° to 115°) water
1 package active dry yeast
Pinch of sugar
¼ cup vegetable shortening
2 tablespoons plus 2 teaspoons hot water

About 2 cups flour
1 teaspoon salt
¼ teaspoon baking soda
¼ teaspoon cream of tartar

1. Place the lukewarm water in a small bowl and sprinkle the yeast over it. Stir in the sugar and let stand until the yeast begins to foam, about 5 minutes.

2. In another bowl, beat together the vegetable shortening and the hot water.

3. In a medium bowl, stir together 1½ cups of the flour, the salt, baking soda, and cream of tartar, and make a well in the center. Pour in the yeast mixture and the shortening mixture, and stir vigorously until smooth. Beat in up to ½ cup more flour to form a dough.

4. Transfer the dough to a lightly floured surface and knead it for about 5 minutes, adding a bit more flour, if necessary, to keep it from sticking. Form the dough into a

Honey-Graham Crackers

ball and place it in a greased bowl. Cover the bowl with plastic wrap, place it in the refrigerator, and let the dough rest for at least 6 hours.

5. Preheat the oven to 425°.

6. Lightly grease a baking sheet. Divide the dough into two portions. On a lightly floured surface, using a floured rolling pin, roll out one portion of dough to an 11 x 6-inch rectangle. With a short side of the rectangle toward you, fold it into thirds, like a letter, bringing the bottom and top over the center to make three layers. Roll out the dough again, forming a rectangle about 11 x 8 inches.

7. Using a ruler and a sharp knife, cut the dough into 16 rectangles, then prick them with a fork. Or, use a small cookie cutter to cut rounds or other shapes.

8. Transfer the crackers to the prepared baking sheet, placing them close together but not touching, and bake for 8 to 10 minutes, or until very lightly browned; watch carefully to be sure they do not brown too much. Cool the crackers on a rack. Shape and bake the second portion of dough.   *Makes 32*

Honey-Graham Crackers

Perennial childhood favorites, graham crackers may be made with whole-wheat flour or with the slightly coarser graham flour. Since whole-grain flours are more perishable than refined products, they should be kept in the refrigerator or freezer.

⅓ cup butter, softened to room temperature	1 teaspoon baking soda
¼ cup (packed) light brown sugar	¼ cup honey
1 egg	1½ to 2 cups whole-wheat flour
1 tablespoon milk	1 cup all-purpose flour
	¼ teaspoon salt

1. Preheat the oven to 375°.

2. In a medium bowl, beat the butter, sugar, and egg together until smooth and creamy.

3. In a small bowl, stir together the milk and baking soda, then add them to the butter mixture. Add the honey and stir to combine. Add 1½ cups of the whole-wheat flour, the all-purpose flour, and the salt, and stir until the mixture forms a dough, adding up to ½ cup more whole-wheat flour if the dough is too sticky. Form the dough into a ball and divide it into 4 portions.

4. Liberally dust a baking sheet with whole-wheat flour. Place one portion of dough on the baking sheet and roll it out to a rectangle roughly 9 x 4½ inches, then use a ruler to trim it to the exact measurement. With a knife, score the dough, without cutting all the way through, into eight 2¼-inch squares. Prick each square with the tines of a fork, or mark it (do not cut all the way through) with a small cookie cutter.

5. Bake the crackers for 10 to 12 minutes, or until golden. Cool the crackers on the baking sheet for 2 to 3 minutes, then carefully transfer them to a rack to cool completely. Shape and bake the remaining portions of dough.   *Makes 32*

*S*ylvester Graham, born in 1794, was an American dietary reformer and temperance advocate. He believed that certain foods, such as spicy condiments, "enflamed the blood" and caused a frightening variety of ills. Graham crusaded for the use of whole-wheat flour as a purifying agent for body and soul; by the 1840s "Graham bread" had become something of a national food fad. It is the Graham cracker, however, that immortalized his name.

Sourdough Bread

This foolproof sourdough bread is made with yeast; the starter is used primarily for its flavor. The starter must be prepared at least three days in advance, but it can be kept for months in the refrigerator if you are not using it immediately.

SOURDOUGH STARTER
2½ cups flour
2½ cups lukewarm (105° to 115°) water
2 teaspoons sugar
1 package active dry yeast

BREAD
2 cups Sourdough Starter

¼ cup lukewarm (105° to 115°) water
1 package active dry yeast
2 teaspoons sugar
2 teaspoons salt
About 4½ cups flour
2 tablespoons butter, softened to room temperature
2 tablespoons cornmeal

1. Make the starter: At least three days before you plan to bake the bread, in a large glass jar stir together the flour, water, sugar, and yeast until well combined. Loosely cover the jar and let stand in a warm, draft-free place for 3 to 5 days, stirring once a day with a wooden spoon. If you are not using the starter as soon as it is ready, cover it tightly and refrigerate. The starter should smell pleasantly sour, and should be thick and filled with small bubbles; if it is not, the yeast is not working and you should begin again with fresh yeast.

2. Make the bread: If the starter has been refrigerated, measure out 2 cups into a large bowl and let it stand at room temperature for 2 hours.

3. Place the water in a small bowl and sprinkle the yeast over it. Let the mixture stand until the yeast dissolves, about 5 minutes.

4. Add the yeast mixture, the sugar, and salt to the room-temperature starter and stir to combine. Stir in 4½ cups of the flour and continue stirring until the mixture forms a dough, adding up to ½ cup more flour if necessary.

5. Beat in the butter. Transfer the dough to a lightly floured surface and knead until smooth and elastic, about 10 minutes. Form the dough into a ball and place it in a large greased bowl. Cover the bowl with a slightly dampened kitchen towel, set it aside in a warm, draft-free place, and let the dough rise until it doubles in bulk, about 1½ hours.

6. Sprinkle a baking sheet lightly with cornmeal. Punch the dough down, then transfer it to a lightly floured surface. Knead the dough lightly for 1 to 2 minutes. Divide the dough into two portions.

7. Shape each piece of dough into a loaf about 8 x 4 inches. Place the loaves on the prepared baking sheet and sprinkle them lightly with flour. Using kitchen scissors, make a zigzag line of deep cuts lengthwise along the top of each loaf.

8. Brush the tops of the loaves with a little water, and set aside, uncovered, to rise in a warm, draft-free place until doubled in bulk, 35 to 45 minutes.

9. Preheat the oven to 375°. Bake the bread for 30 minutes, or until the crusts are well browned and the loaves sound hollow when thumped on the bottom.

Makes two 8-inch loaves

ALASKAN SOURDOUGH

"Sourdoughs" finishing a meal along the Yukon Trail, Dyea Valley, Alaska, in 1897.

They were called "Sourdoughs" —the Alaska Gold Rush prospectors who forged northward in the 1890s. Their spartan sustenance consisted mainly of what they could gather or trap, along with bacon, beans, and sourdough breads and hotcakes.

To prepare the sourdough "starter," flour and water were combined in an open crock. Wild yeasts from the air "soured" (fermented) the mixture, which could then be used as leavening. The starter could be kept "alive" for years if it was replenished with flour and water as it was used.

Sourdough was a necessity in the Klondike because food supplies were so unpredictable. Starter provided a constant, reliable source of leavening, and it could be shared—a valuable gift. Although starter can withstand freezing, it was guarded carefully from the cold to keep it ready for use: A shelf near the stovepipe was reserved for the starter crock, but some "Sourdoughs" took the crock to bed with them to keep it warm.

To keep the starter well protected on treks out of camp, it was sometimes mixed with flour to form a ball of dough, which was then buried in a flour sack. Adept cooks could mix biscuit dough right inside the sack by kneading in more flour.

Sourdough baked goods sustained not only the prospectors, but also their pack animals and sled dogs. In addition, sourdough starter served as a soothing plaster for sprains, as a glue, and as a metal polish. The liquid from the top of the crock, allowed to ferment further, became a strong, admittedly unpalatable liquor known as "hooch."

Today, sourdough bakers prize the tradition—as well as the versatility—of this leavening process. The updated recipe for Sourdough Bread, opposite, will give you the flavor and texture associated with this authentic American bread.

Cheese Sticks

These attractive twists of rich dough are also known as cheese straws. The combination of sharp Cheddar, paprika, and cayenne give the sticks a sharp, tangy flavor, making them ideal for serving with cocktails or as an accompaniment to soups and salads.

1 cup flour
½ teaspoon paprika
½ teaspoon salt
¼ teaspoon baking soda
¼ teaspoon cream of tartar
Pinch of cayenne pepper

⅓ cup chilled butter, cut into pieces
2 tablespoons vegetable shortening
1 cup grated sharp Cheddar cheese
  (about 4 ounces)
2 tablespoons milk

1. In a large bowl, stir together the flour, paprika, salt, baking soda, cream of tartar, and cayenne. Using a pastry blender or two knives, cut in the butter and vegetable shortening until the mixture resembles coarse crumbs.

2. Stir in the cheese, then add the milk and stir just until the mixture forms a cohesive dough. Cover the bowl with plastic wrap and refrigerate for at least 1 hour.

3. Preheat the oven to 425°.

4. Lightly grease a baking sheet. Transfer the dough to a lightly floured surface. Using a lightly floured rolling pin, roll out the dough to a 12 x 4-inch rectangle. Cut twenty-four 4 x ½-inch strips. Twist each strip lengthwise, then place all of them on the prepared baking sheet. Bake for 10 to 12 minutes, or until golden around the edges. Transfer the cheese sticks to a rack to cool completely.   *Makes 2 dozen*

Raisin-Walnut Pumpernickel

Unlike dense, chewy Russian pumpernickel, this bread has a relatively light texture and a sweet flavor, similar to that of Swedish limpa bread.

1½ cups lukewarm (105° to 115°) water
2 packages active dry yeast
1 tablespoon granulated sugar
2 tablespoons plus 1 teaspoon instant
  coffee
3 cups rye flour
About 2 cups all-purpose flour
1 cup raisins

1 cup chopped walnuts
¼ cup (packed) dark brown sugar
3 tablespoons molasses
3 tablespoons butter, melted
1 teaspoon salt
1 egg yolk
1 tablespoon milk

1. Place ¼ cup of the water in a large bowl and sprinkle the yeast over it. Stir in the granulated sugar and let stand until the yeast begins to foam, about 5 minutes.

2. In a small bowl, dissolve 2 tablespoons of the instant coffee in the remaining 1¼ cups water.

3. Add the dissolved coffee, the rye flour, 1½ cups of the all-purpose flour, the raisins, walnuts, brown sugar, molasses, butter, and salt to the yeast mixture, and stir to form a dough. Add up to ½ cup more all-purpose flour if the dough is too sticky. Transfer the dough to a lightly floured surface and knead it for 1 or 2 minutes, then let the dough rest, uncovered, for 10 minutes.

4. Knead the dough until smooth and elastic, about 10 minutes, then form it into a ball and transfer it to a large greased bowl. Cover the bowl with a slightly dampened kitchen towel, set it aside in a warm, draft-free place, and let the dough rise until it doubles in bulk, 45 minutes to 1 hour.

5. Lightly grease a large baking sheet. Punch the dough down, divide it in half, and shape it into two round loaves. Place the loaves several inches apart on the prepared baking sheet. Set aside, uncovered, in a warm, draft-free place to rise until doubled in bulk, about 45 minutes.

6. Preheat the oven to 375°. In a small bowl, beat the egg yolk with the milk and the remaining 1 teaspoon instant coffee to make a glaze.

7. Brush the tops of the loaves with the glaze and bake for 40 to 45 minutes, or until the loaves sound hollow when thumped on the bottom. Cool the breads on the baking sheet for 10 minutes, then transfer them to a rack to cool completely before slicing.

Makes two 8-inch loaves

Sesame Seed Biscuits

A quick hand and a light touch are prerequisites for tender biscuits. For best results, stir in the liquid just until it is incorporated, and knead the dough very briefly.

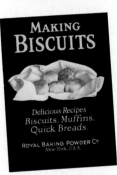

⅓ cup sesame seeds	½ teaspoon salt
2 cups flour	3 tablespoons chilled butter,
2 teaspoons baking powder	cut into pieces
½ teaspoon baking soda	1 cup heavy cream

1. Preheat the oven to 400°. Meanwhile, place the sesame seeds in a small ungreased skillet and toast them over medium heat, shaking the pan frequently, until golden, 10 to 14 minutes. Set aside to cool slightly.

2. In a medium bowl, stir together the flour, baking powder, baking soda, salt, and toasted sesame seeds. Using a pastry blender or two knives, cut in the butter until the mixture resembles coarse crumbs.

3. Gradually add the cream, stirring with a fork just until the dough holds together. Transfer the dough to a lightly floured surface and knead it for 1 minute. Using a lightly floured rolling pin, roll the dough out to a ½-inch thickness. With a 2-inch round biscuit cutter, cut out 24 biscuits. Gather, reroll, and cut any scraps.

4. Place the biscuits on an ungreased cookie sheet and bake for 10 to 12 minutes, or until light golden. Transfer the biscuits to a rack to cool briefly. Serve warm.

Makes about 2 dozen

Pull-Apart Dinner Rolls

Hot, homemade dinner rolls may be one of life's little luxuries, but they are quite easy to make. This recipe can be baked as a panful of attractive pull-apart rolls (as shown at left), or the dough can be formed into a variety of shapes, such as cloverleafs, crescents, or buttery, multilayered fans. See Shaped Dinner Rolls, pages 160-161, for step-by-step photos.

¾ cup boiling water
⅓ cup nonfat dry milk
¼ cup lukewarm (105° to 115°) water
1 package active dry yeast
2 tablespoons sugar
About 3¼ cups flour
½ teaspoon salt

2 eggs
2 tablespoons butter, softened to
*   room temperature*
2 tablespoons milk
2 tablespoons sesame seeds
*   or poppy seeds*

1. In a small bowl, stir together the boiling water and nonfat dry milk. Set aside to cool to lukewarm (105° to 115°).

2. Place the lukewarm water in another small bowl and sprinkle the yeast over it. Stir in a pinch of the sugar and let stand until the yeast begins to foam, about 5 minutes.

3. In a large bowl, stir together 2¾ cups of the flour, the remaining sugar, and the salt, and make a well in the center. Pour in the lukewarm milk mixture, the yeast mixture, and one of the eggs, and stir until smooth.

4. Gradually beat in the butter. Continue to beat until the butter is incorporated and the mixture forms a soft dough.

5. Transfer the dough to a lightly floured surface and knead it until smooth and elastic, about 10 minutes, adding up to ½ cup more flour, if necessary, to keep the dough from sticking. Form the dough into a ball and place it in a large greased bowl. Cover the bowl with a slightly dampened kitchen towel, set it aside in a warm, draft-free place, and let the dough rise until it doubles in bulk, 45 minutes to 1 hour.

6. Lightly grease a 9-inch round cake pan. Punch the dough down, then transfer it to a lightly floured surface. Knead the dough lightly for 1 to 2 minutes. Divide the dough into 20 equal portions and roll each into a ball.

7. Starting from the center, place the balls in concentric rings around the prepared pan. Set aside, uncovered, in a warm, draft-free place to rise until almost doubled in bulk, about 30 minutes.

8. Preheat the oven to 425°. In a small bowl, beat together the remaining egg and the milk to make a glaze.

9. Brush the tops of the rolls with the egg glaze, sprinkle them with the sesame seeds, and bake for 12 to 15 minutes, or until golden on top. Let the rolls cool in the pan for 5 minutes, then run the tip of a knife around the edges of the pan to loosen the rolls, turn them out of the pan, and serve warm.   *Makes 20*

Pull-Apart Dinner Rolls

SHAPED DINNER ROLLS

CLOVERLEAF ROLLS

These rolls are made with the same dough used for the Pull-Apart Dinner Rolls on page 159. After the first rising (Step 5 of the recipe), punch the dough down, knead it briefly, and follow the method described at right. For variations on these rolls, employ the same technique, but instead of three balls, use four to create a four-leaf clover, or just two large balls to make a roll resembling a Parker House.

Divide the dough into four equal portions. Roll each portion roughly into a thick rope and, with a sharp knife, cut each dough rope into nine equal pieces.

Roll each of the pieces of dough into a small ball. The balls do not have to be perfectly round; they will fill out and become smooth as they rise.

CRESCENT ROLLS

Although shaped like croissants, crescent rolls are much easier to make. Use the recipe for Pull-Apart Dinner Rolls on page 159, and after the first rising (Step 5), punch the dough down, knead briefly, and follow the method described at right. The rolls can also be transformed into breakfast pastries: make them twice as big as instructed here and sprinkle the buttered dough with cinnamon-sugar before rolling them up.

Divide the dough into two equal portions and form them into balls. Roll each ball out to a 12-inch circle. Make the circle as even and symmetrical as possible.

Brush each dough circle generously with melted butter, using at least 1 tablespoon of butter for each circle. The butter makes the rolls richer.

FAN ROLLS

These delicious buttery rolls are made by baking seven thin layers of dough together in one muffin cup. Melted butter prevents the layers from sticking together and makes the roll fun to pull apart and eat. Use the recipe for Pull-Apart Dinner Rolls on page 159, and after the first rising (Step 5), punch the dough down, turn it out onto a floured work surface, knead it briefly, and follow the technique described at right.

Halve the dough and roll it into two 12 x 10½-inch rectangles. Brush with melted butter and then cut each rectangle lengthwise into seven strips.

Stack the seven strips on top of one another. Take care not to let the strips stretch out as you lift them off the work surface, or the stack will not be uniform.

Roll the balls in melted butter and place three of them in each of 12 muffin cups. Set aside, uncovered, in a warm, draft-free place to rise until almost doubled.

Brush the rolls with egg glaze (1 whole egg beaten with 2 tablespoons milk) and, if desired, sprinkle the tops with sesame seeds or poppy seeds.

Bake the rolls at 425° for about 12 minutes, or until the tops are golden brown. As with all dinner rolls, these are best served warm from the oven.

With a sharp knife, cut each dough circle into quarters. Then cut each quarter into thirds to make 12 wedges per circle, for a total of 24 wedges.

Starting at the wide end, roll up each wedge and place it on a greased baking sheet. Curve the pointed ends slightly toward one another to make crescents.

Let rise, uncovered, in a warm, draft-free place until almost doubled. Brush with egg glaze and bake at 425° for about 12 minutes, or until golden brown on top.

With a sharp knife, cut each stack into 2-inch segments. If any of the layers are stuck together, gently pry them apart so the roll will fan out when baked.

Place the rolls in greased muffin cups, with the cut edges up. Set the rolls aside, uncovered, in a warm, draft-free place to rise until almost doubled.

Brush the rolls lightly with egg glaze (1 whole egg beaten with 2 tablespoons milk). Bake at 425° for about 12 minutes, or until the tops are golden brown.

Five-Grain Loaf

This flavorful, firm-textured bread, perfect for hearty sandwiches, contains rye, cornmeal, millet, oats, and wheat (in three different forms). Whole-wheat flour and wheat germ can be found in most supermarkets; wheat "flakes," which are rolled wheat berries and resemble rolled oats, are sold in health-food stores.

2 cups lukewarm (105° to 115°) water
1 package active dry yeast
Pinch of sugar
¼ cup honey
2 tablespoons light vegetable oil, such as safflower
About 3 cups whole-wheat flour
1 cup rye flour

1 cup yellow cornmeal
½ cup hulled millet
½ cup wheat germ
2 teaspoons salt
6 tablespoons old-fashioned rolled oats
6 tablespoons roasted sunflower seeds
6 tablespoons wheat flakes
1 egg white, lightly beaten

1. Place ¼ cup of the water in a small bowl and sprinkle the yeast over it. Stir in the sugar and let stand until the yeast begins to foam, about 5 minutes

2. In a medium bowl, stir together the honey, oil, and remaining 1¾ cups water.

3. In a large bowl, stir together 2½ cups of the whole-wheat flour, the rye flour, cornmeal, millet, wheat germ, salt, and 4 tablespoons each of the rolled oats, sunflower seeds, and wheat flakes.

4. Add the yeast mixture and the honey mixture to the dry ingredients, and stir to form a slightly sticky dough. Transfer the dough to a lightly floured surface and knead until smooth, about 10 minutes, adding up to ½ cup more whole-wheat flour if necessary.

5. Form the dough into a ball and transfer it to a large greased bowl. Cover the bowl with a slightly dampened kitchen towel, set it aside in a warm, draft-free place, and let the dough rise until it doubles in bulk, 45 minutes to 1 hour.

6. Lightly grease two 8 x 4½-inch loaf pans. Punch the dough down, then transfer it to a lightly floured surface and knead it lightly for 1 minute. Divide the dough in half, form it into two loaves, each about 8 x 4 inches, and place them in the prepared pans. Set aside, uncovered, in a warm, draft-free place to rise until almost doubled in bulk, 30 to 45 minutes.

7. Preheat the oven to 425°. In a small bowl, combine the remaining 2 tablespoons each rolled oats, sunflower seeds, and wheat flakes. Brush the tops of the loaves with the egg white and sprinkle with the sunflower-grain mixture, pressing gently so it adheres to the dough.

8. Bake the loaves for 10 minutes, then reduce the oven temperature to 325° and bake for another 30 to 40 minutes, or until the loaves are golden brown and sound hollow when thumped on the bottom. Cool the loaves in the pans for 10 minutes, then turn them out onto a rack to cool completely before slicing.   *Makes two 8-inch loaves*

The 1910 book *Light Entertaining* stated that "The old-fashioned sandwich, which consisted of a slice of cold meat laid between two slices of buttered bread, has little in common with the sandwich of today. Nowadays sandwich-making is a veritable art. . . . Wheat, rye, graham, entire wheat or brown bread may all be used . . . but discretion must be used as to just what particular filling combines best with these different varieties of bread."

Five-Grain Loaf

Cream-Cheese Biscuits

These biscuits can be made in any size. For example, two-inch miniature biscuits, filled with ham or smoked turkey, make tempting hors d'oeuvres.

About 1½ cups flour
¾ cup yellow cornmeal
2 teaspoons baking powder
½ teaspoon salt
3 ounces chilled cream cheese,
* cut into pieces*

3 tablespoons chilled butter, cut
* into pieces*
1 egg, lightly beaten
About ⅓ cup buttermilk, or ⅓ cup
* milk plus 1 teaspoon vinegar*

1. Preheat the oven to 450°.
2. In a medium bowl, stir together 1½ cups of the flour, the cornmeal, baking powder, and salt. Using a pastry blender or two knives, cut in the cream cheese and butter until the mixture resembles coarse crumbs.
3. Stir in the egg, then stir in just enough buttermilk to form a dough.
4. Transfer the dough to a lightly floured surface and knead it for 1 to 2 minutes, adding up to 2 tablespoons more flour if it is too sticky. Roll out the dough to a ½-inch thickness. With a 3-inch round biscuit cutter, cut out 8 biscuits. Gather, reroll, and cut any scraps.
5. Place the biscuits on an ungreased baking sheet and bake for 12 to 15 minutes, or until pale golden brown on top. Serve hot. *Makes about 10*

Angel Biscuits

This recipe is also called Bride's Biscuits because the use of yeast, in addition to baking soda, guarantees light biscuits, even for novice cooks.

2 tablespoons lukewarm (105° to 115°)
* water*
1 package active dry yeast
1 tablespoon sugar
2½ cups flour

½ teaspoon baking soda
½ teaspoon salt
⅓ cup chilled butter, cut into tablespoons
1 cup buttermilk, or 1 cup milk plus
* 1 tablespoon vinegar*

1. Place the water in a small bowl and sprinkle the yeast over it. Add a pinch of the sugar and let stand until the yeast begins to foam, about 5 minutes.
2. In a medium bowl, stir together the flour, the remaining sugar, the baking soda, and salt. Using a pastry blender or two knives, cut in the butter until the mixture resembles coarse meal.
3. Add the buttermilk and then the yeast mixture, and stir just until a soft dough forms. Transfer the dough to a lightly floured surface and knead until smooth, about 2 minutes. Form the dough into a ball and place it in a large greased bowl. Cover the bowl

with a slightly dampened kitchen towel, set it aside in a warm, draft-free place, and let the dough rise until it doubles in bulk, 45 minutes to 1 hour.

4. Punch the dough down, then transfer it to a lightly floured surface. Using a lightly floured rolling pin, roll out the dough to a ½-inch thickness. With a 2-inch round biscuit cutter, cut out 24 biscuits. Gather, reroll, and cut any scraps.

5. Place the biscuits on an ungreased baking sheet and set aside, uncovered, in a warm, draft-free place to rise until almost doubled in bulk, about 30 minutes.

6. Preheat the oven to 400°. Bake the biscuits for 10 to 12 minutes, or until golden brown. Serve hot.

Makes about 2 dozen

Rye Beer Bread

This recipe is popular in Milwaukee, where descendants of German immigrants make good use of an important local product—beer—to flavor their earthy rye bread.

¼ cup lukewarm (105° to 115°) water
1 package active dry yeast
Pinch of sugar
About 3½ cups all-purpose flour
2 cups rye flour
¾ cup yellow cornmeal

4 tablespoons plus 1 teaspoon caraway seeds
2 teaspoons salt
1½ cups (12 ounces) dark beer
2 tablespoons butter, melted
2 tablespoons molasses
1 egg white, lightly beaten

1. Place the water in a small bowl and sprinkle the yeast over it. Stir in the sugar, and let the mixture stand until the yeast begins to foam, about 5 minutes.

2. In a large bowl, stir together 3 cups of the all-purpose flour, the rye flour, cornmeal, 3 tablespoons of the caraway seeds, the salt, and the yeast mixture. Stir in the beer, butter, and molasses. The dough should be somewhat sticky, but if it is very sticky, add up to ¼ cup more all-purpose flour.

3. Transfer the dough to a lightly floured surface and knead it until smooth and elastic, about 10 minutes, adding up to ¼ cup more flour if the dough is very sticky. Form the dough into a ball and place it in a large greased bowl. Cover the bowl with a slightly dampened kitchen towel, set it aside in a warm, draft-free place, and let the dough rise until it doubles in bulk, 1½ to 2 hours.

4. Preheat the oven to 375°. Lightly grease a large baking sheet.

5. Punch the dough down, then transfer it to a lightly floured surface and knead it lightly for 1 minute. Divide the dough in half. Shape each piece of dough into an oval loaf about 9 inches long and place the loaves on the prepared baking sheet.

6. Brush the loaves with the egg white and sprinkle the tops with the remaining 4 teaspoons caraway seeds; press the seeds lightly into the dough. Bake for 35 to 40 minutes, or until the loaves are golden brown and sound hollow when thumped on the bottom. Cool the loaves on the baking sheet for 1 to 2 minutes, then transfer them to a rack to cool completely before slicing.

Makes two 9-inch loaves

Bacon-Cheese Biscuits

Cutting biscuits into squares saves time and effort—there are no scraps to reroll and cut. Serve these biscuits for breakfast, or with soup for lunch.

3 slices bacon
About 2 cups flour
2 teaspoons baking powder
½ teaspoon baking soda
¼ teaspoon pepper

4 tablespoons chilled butter, cut into
  pieces
1 cup grated Monterey jack cheese
  (about 4 ounces)
¾ cup milk

1. Preheat the oven to 425°. In a skillet, cook the bacon over medium heat until crisp, about 10 minutes. Drain the bacon on paper towels; set aside.

2. In a medium bowl, stir together 2 cups of the flour, the baking powder, baking soda, and pepper. Using a pastry blender or two knives, cut in the butter until the mixture resembles coarse crumbs.

3. Crumble in the bacon, then add the cheese and milk, and stir briefly to form a dough. Transfer the dough to a lightly floured surface and knead for 1 to 2 minutes, adding up to 2 tablespoons more flour if necessary.

4. Roll out the dough to a rectangle roughly 9 x 7 inches. With a floured knife, cut the rectangle into twelve 2¼-inch squares.

5. Place the biscuits on an ungreased baking sheet and bake for 12 to 15 minutes, or until golden. Serve hot.

Makes 1 dozen

Potato Bread

Making bread with potatoes—either white or sweet—is not a newfangled idea. Early recipes for homemade yeast or "starter" were often based on potatoes or potato cooking water. Here, both warm mashed potato and its cooking liquid are used to produce a light, moist bread with a delicious crisp crust.

1 large boiling potato (about 8 ounces), peeled and coarsely chopped	⅓ cup sugar
1 cup milk	2 eggs, lightly beaten
1 package active dry yeast	½ teaspoon salt
	About 5½ cups flour

Marion Harland's Common Sense in the Household *offered that author's usual authoritative advice for kneading bread: "Knead hard—always toward the centre of the mass, which should be repeatedly turned over and around, that every portion may be manipulated. Brisk and long kneading makes the pores fine and regular. . . . Spend at least twenty minutes— half an hour is better—in this kind of useful gymnastics. It is grand exercise for arms and chest."*

1. Place the chopped potato in a small saucepan and add water to cover. Cook over medium heat until tender, 15 to 20 minutes. Drain the potato, reserving ¼ cup of the cooking liquid. Set the liquid aside to cool to lukewarm (105° to 115°).

2. Meanwhile, in a small saucepan, scald the milk. Remove the pan from the heat and let the milk cool to lukewarm (105° to 115°).

3. Sprinkle the yeast over the lukewarm potato cooking liquid and let stand until the yeast dissolves, about 5 minutes

4. Mash the potato. Transfer ¾ cup of the mashed potato to a large bowl. Stir in the lukewarm milk, the yeast mixture, and the sugar.

5. Beat in the eggs and salt. Add 2½ cups of the flour and beat well. Add another 2½ cups of flour and beat well.

6. Transfer the dough to a lightly floured surface and knead until soft but not sticky, about 10 minutes, adding up to ½ cup more flour if necessary to keep the dough from sticking. Form the dough into a ball and place it in a large greased bowl. Cover the bowl with a slightly dampened kitchen towel, set it aside in a warm, draft-free place, and let the dough rise until it doubles in bulk, 1 to 1¼ hours.

7. Lightly grease 2 large baking sheets. Punch the dough down, then transfer it to a lightly floured surface. Knead the dough lightly for 1 to 2 minutes. Divide the dough into two portions and form each into a round loaf about 6 inches in diameter.

8. Place each loaf on a prepared baking sheet. Set aside, uncovered, in a warm, draft-free place to rise until doubled in bulk, about 1 hour.

9. Preheat the oven to 375°. Using a single-edged razor blade, slash the top of one loaf at ¾-inch intervals in a checkerboard pattern. Dust the loaf with about 1 teaspoon of flour. (Cover the second loaf loosely with plastic wrap and leave it in the refrigerator until ready to bake, but no longer than 1 hour.)

10. Bake the bread for 25 to 30 minutes, or until the loaf is golden brown on top and sounds hollow when thumped on the bottom.

11. Let the baked loaf cool on the baking sheet for 10 minutes, then transfer it to a rack to cool completely. Meanwhile, slash, flour, and bake the second loaf.

Makes two 9-inch round loaves

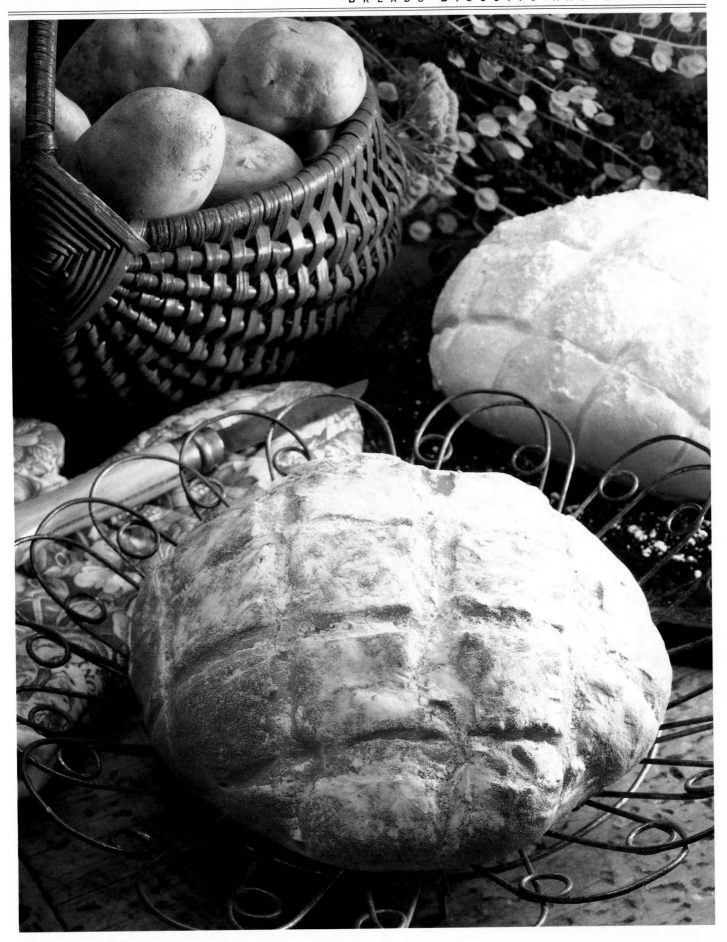

Photography and Illustration Credits

All photographs by Christopher Lawrence, except the following: Frontispiece and pages 14-15, 19, 26, 27, 34, 35, 38, 54-55, 63, 70-71, 82-83, 88-89, 98-99, 106-107, 116-117, 124-125, 132-133, 146, 147, 160-161: Steven Mays. Page 62 and all marginal photographs of promotional recipe booklets: Rob Whitcomb. Pages 62-63: border illustrations and design by Amy Berniker. Page 155: courtesy of the Library of Congress.

Prop Credits

The Editors would like to thank the following for their courtesy in lending items for photography. Items not listed below are privately owned. **Frontispiece:** heart and hand cookie cutter—K. Dunwoody Tinsmith, Quarryville, PA. **Page 8:** pie crimper, rolling pin, and wooden scoop—LaVerne Yakel Antiques, Woodbury, CT. **Pages 10-11:** antique sideboard and majolica plates—West Country Antiques, Woodbury, CT; majolica compote and sterling silver forks—Grass Roots, Woodbury, CT. **Pages 14-15:** glass rolling pin collection courtesy of Rita Entmacher Cohen, Closter, NJ; canvas tablecloth—Zweigart Canvas ® courtesy of Joan Toggitt, Ltd., West Caldwell, NJ. **Page 16:** all props—Grass Roots, Woodbury, CT. **Page 19:** wallcovering, "Shirt Stripe" #K145—Laura Ashley, NYC; basket—Sheila Gelb, New Hyde Park, NY. **Page 23:** wood surface—Woodbury Barn Antiques, Woodbury, CT; antique metal plate—West Country Antiques, Woodbury, CT. **Pages 24-25:** cutting board and pie rack—Ann Beckman, Woodbury, CT. **Page 26:** (top) pie basket and fabric—The Watermelon Patch, Manhasset, NY; tiles, "Amarrado," in crosses, buds, and bullnoses, #412—Country Floors, NYC; crocheted cloth—Primrose Lane, Manhasset, NY; (bottom) basket and napkin—The Watermelon Patch. **Page 27:** (top) cloth, "Orchard" #K198—Laura Ashley, NYC; basket—The Watermelon Patch, Manhasset, NY; (bottom) basket—The Watermelon Patch; eyelet napkin—Primrose Lane, Manhasset, NY. **Page 30:** pink Depression glass cake plate—Grass Roots, Woodbury, CT. **Pages 32-33:** basket—Country Bazaar, Woodbury, CT; glassware—by Mariposa, courtesy of Palmer Smith, NYC. **Page 35:** wallcovering, "Williamsburg Apples"—Katzenbach & Warren, Inc., Cleveland; yellowware bowls and potholders—Roslyn House Antiques, Roslyn, NY; nutmeg grater—Primrose Lane, Manhasset, NY; blue stoneware bowl—The Watermelon Patch, Manhasset, NY. **Page 38:** wicker chair and table—The Wicker Garden, NYC; hot chocolate cups and saucers—Primrose Lane, Manhasset, NY; green goblet—Sheila Gelb, New Hyde Park, NY; chintz tablecloth—The Watermelon Patch, Manhasset, NY. **Page 44:** cake plate, demitasse cups and saucers, flatware, dessert plates, nut bowl, and linens—Grass Roots, Woodbury, CT; table—West Country Antiques, Woodbury, CT. **Page 47:** dessert plate—Palmer Smith, NYC; hand-painted surface by Sara Barbaris. **Page 57:** plates and vase—Fishs Eddy, NYC; wallcovering, "Ambersham Arms" #AA802-W, from The Tilling Collection—Raintree Designs, Inc., NYC; ice cream chair—Primrose Lane, Manhasset, NY. **Page 58:** plate—Grass Roots, Woodbury, CT; chair—West Country Antiques, Woodbury, CT. **Pages 62-63:** Pillsbury Bake-Off booklets—Kitchen Arts & Letters, NYC. **Page 68:** ironstone cake plate—West Country Antiques, Woodbury, CT. **Pages 70-71:** spice containers from the collections of: Pantry and Hearth Antiques, NYC; Meryle Evans, NYC; Alice Ross Hearth Studio, Inc., Smithtown, NY; Primrose Lane, Manhasset, NY; Phyllis Wrynn, Brooklyn, NY. **Page 73:** Depression glass plate—Grass Roots, Woodbury, CT. **Page 76:** wire fruit basket—Grass Roots, Woodbury, CT; oak table and Irish pine shelves—West Country Antiques, Woodbury, CT. **Page 78:** woodenware collection—Nancy Fierberg Antiques, Woodbury, CT. **Pages 82-83:** large round terra-cotta mold—Williams-Sonoma, San Francisco, CA; rocking horse, cow, and Victorian heart cookie molds—Hill Design, Inc., Manchester, NH; basket of flowers, fox family, mama bear, baby bear, lamb, and sweet shop cookie molds—Hartstone, Inc., Zanesville, OH; cast-iron rolling cookie mold and all antique wooden cookie molds—Alice Ross Hearth Studio, Inc., Smithtown, NY; cast-iron George Washington cookie mold—Meryle Evans, NYC; fabric—The Watermelon Patch, Manhasset, NY. **Page 84:** linens—The Brass Ring, Woodbury, CT. **Pages 88-89:** fabric—The Watermelon Patch, Manhasset, NY. **Page 91:** silver compote and spoons—Grass Roots, Woodbury, CT. **Page 92:** wallcovering, "Square Dance" #KAV-140, from Kitchen and Bath—Motif Designs, New Rochelle, NY; plates—Fishs Eddy, NYC. **Pages 96-97:** wood surface—West Country Antiques, Woodbury, CT. **Page 99:** (middle) blue-and-white tea cloth—Pantry and Hearth Antiques, NYC. **Page 100:** pottery—MacKenzie Childs, Ltd., Aurora, NY. **Pages 106-107:** cookie jars—Kaleidoscope Antiques, NYC. **Page 108:** lace runner—The Brass Ring, Woodbury, CT. **Page 111:** enamel tea kettle—Grass Roots, Woodbury, CT. **Pages 116-117:** tin muffin pans—Pantry and Hearth Antiques, NYC; cast-iron muffin pans—Joel Schiff, NYC. **Page 127:** dessert plate—West Country Antiques, Woodbury, CT; mugs—Grass

Roots, Woodbury, CT. **Page 128**: hand-painted box by Robert G. Williams, Woodbury, CT. **Page 133**: fabrics—Pierre Deux, NYC. **Pages 144-145**: hand-painted cupboard and sugar bowl—Church Street Trading, New Milford, CT. **Page 146**: wallcovering, "Dorset," Williamsburg reproduction—Katzenbach & Warren, Inc., Cleveland; table—Pine Country Antiques, NYC. **Page 151**: Fiestaware, salt box, cookie jar, flatware, and linens—Beverly's Collectibles, Brookfield, CT; toaster—Southbury Antiques Center, Southbury, CT. **Page 161**: (bottom) embroidered linen and silver spoon—Primrose Lane, Manhasset, NY. **Page 162**: wallcovering, "Williamsburg Apples"—Katzenbach & Warren, Inc., Cleveland; painting and table—West Country Antiques, Woodbury, CT; napkin—Church Street Trading, New Milford, CT. **Page 169**: painted basket—Nancy Fierberg Antiques, Woodbury, CT.

Index

Acknowledgments

Our thanks to the American Gas Association, Mary Smith Carson, Rita Entmacher Cohen, Marlene Johnson, Gene Palm, The Pillsbury Company, Joel Schiff, and Phyllis Steiss Wetherill for their help on this book. CleanTop Range courtesy of the Whirlpool Corporation.

© 1990 Time-Life Books Inc. All rights reserved

No part of this book may be reproduced in any form or by any electronic
or mechanical means, including information storage and retrieval devices
or systems, without prior written permission from the publisher
except that brief passages may be quoted for reviews.
First printing
Published simultaneously in Canada
School and library distribution by Silver Burdett Company,
Morristown, New Jersey

TIME-LIFE is a trademark of Time Incorporated U.S.A.

Production by Giga Communications, Inc.
Printed in U.S.A.

Library of Congress Cataloging-in-Publication Data

Country Baking
p.   cm. — (American country)
ISBN 0-8094-6787-9 — ISBN 0-8094-6788-7 (lib. bdg.)
1. Baking—United States.
I. Time-Life Books.   II. Series.
TX763.C68   1990   641.7'1—dc20   90-10773
CIP

American Country was created by Rebus, Inc., and published by Time-Life Books.

REBUS, INC.

Publisher: RODNEY FRIEDMAN • Editor: MARYA DALRYMPLE
Executive Editor: RACHEL D. CARLEY • Managing Editor: BRENDA SAVARD • Consulting Editor: CHARLES L. MEE, JR.
Senior Editor: SUSAN B. GOODMAN • Copy Editor: ALEXA RIPLEY BARRE
Writers: JUDITH CRESSY, ROSEMARY G. RENNICKE
Design Editors: NANCY MERNIT, CATHRYN SCHWING
Editor, The Country Letter: BONNIE J. SLOTNICK
Editorial Assistant: LEE CUTRONE

Art Director: JUDITH HENRY • Associate Art Director: SARA REYNOLDS
Designers: AMY BERNIKER, TIMOTHY JEFFS
Photographer: STEVEN MAYS • Photo Editor: SUE ISRAEL • Photo Assistant: ROB WHITCOMB

Series Consultants: BOB CAHN, HELAINE W. FENDELMAN, LINDA C. FRANKLIN, GLORIA GALE,
KATHLEEN EAGEN JOHNSON, JUNE SPRIGG, CLAIRE WHITCOMB

Staff for *Country Baking*
Editor: KATE SLATE • Senior Editor/Writer: BONNIE J. SLOTNICK
Test Kitchen Director/Food Stylist: GRACE YOUNG • Test Kitchen Associate: MARIE BAKER-LEE
Copy Editor: MARSHA LUTCH LLOYD • Contributing Editor: SANTHA CASSELL
Photographer: CHRISTOPHER LAWRENCE • Photo Stylists: SARA BARBARIS, DEE SHAPIRO
Photo Assistants: RICHARD JOHNSON, GARRY SPENCER WADE
Freelance Writer: MINDY HEIFERLING • Freelance Food Stylist: KAREN HATT

Time-Life Books Inc. is a wholly owned subsidiary of THE TIME INC. BOOK COMPANY.

President and Chief Executive Officer: KELSO F. SUTTON
President, Time Inc. Books Direct: CHRISTOPHER T. LINEN

TIME-LIFE BOOKS INC.

Editor: GEORGE CONSTABLE
Director of Design: LOUIS KLEIN • Director of Editorial Resources: PHYLLIS K. WISE
Director of Photography and Research: JOHN CONRAD WEISER

President: JOHN M. FAHEY JR.
Senior Vice Presidents: ROBERT M. DeSENA, PAUL R. STEWART, CURTIS G. VIEBRANZ, JOSEPH J. WARD
Vice Presidents: STEPHEN L. BAIR, BONITA L. BOEZEMAN, MARY P. DONOHOE, STEPHEN L. GOLDSTEIN,
JUANITA T. JAMES, ANDREW P. KAPLAN, TREVOR LUNN, SUSAN J. MARUYAMA, ROBERT H. SMITH
New Product Development: TREVOR LUNN, DONIA ANN STEELE
Supervisor of Quality Control: JAMES KING

Publisher: JOSEPH J. WARD

For information about any Time-Life book please call 1-800-621-7026, or write:
Reader Information, Time-Life Customer Service
P.O. Box C-32068, Richmond, Virginia 23261-2068

Time-Life Books Inc. offers a wide range of fine recordings, including a Rock 'n' Roll Era series.
For subscription information, call 1-800-621-7026, or write TIME-LIFE MUSIC,
P.O. Box C-32068, Richmond, Virginia 23261-2068.

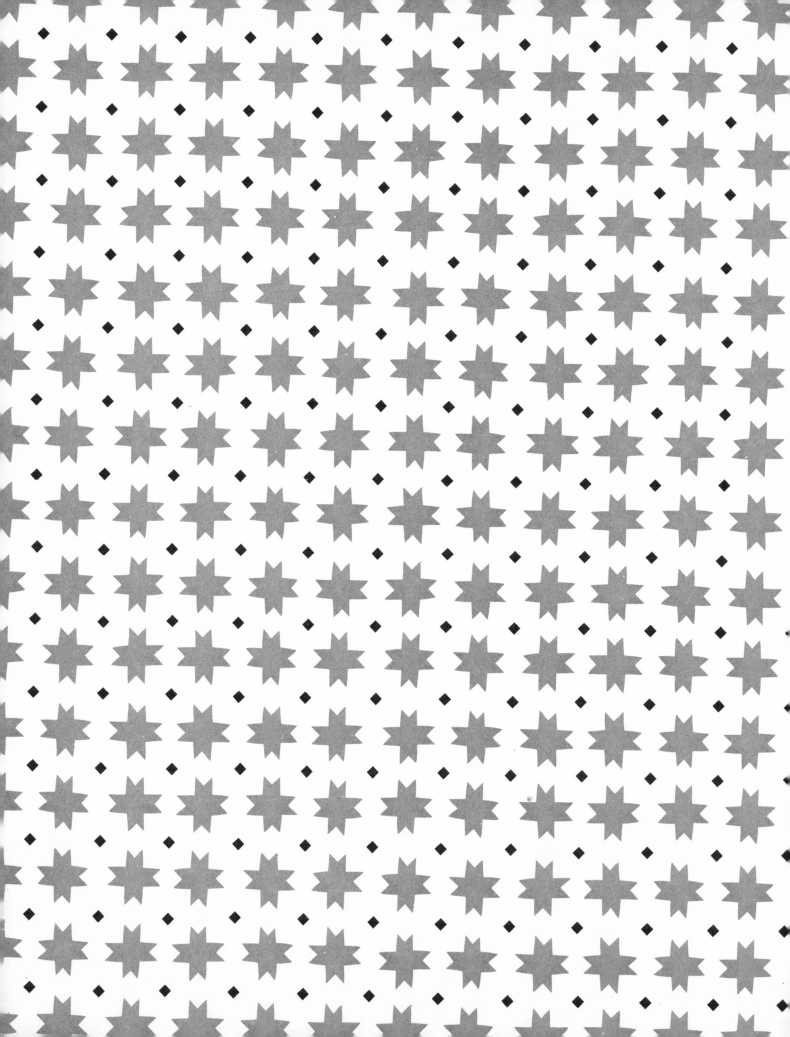